WHERE DO ALL THE MEMORIES GO?

ACKNOWLEDGMENTS:

• After hearing some of my stories repeated several times, some family members, out of self-defense suggested I write a book. The decision to do so came one sleepless night in 1995 while suffering from Shingles. I was wide awake all night so to pass the time I began pulling up childhood memories. As they passed across my mental screen a basic format emerged which has not been changed very much.

• I am grateful to my granddaughter, Tanya Nissley, and Mary Frerking, for ploughing through all this stuff to computerize it; to my daughter, Ruth, and son, Dale, for their genuine interest and generous support; to my sister, Naomi, and her husband, Sandy Limont, for preserving these photos and records over the years and for their untiring efforts at identification, editing and professional layout suggestions; to Susan Miller for sharing her literary skills in checking punctuation and syntax; to Elam Hertzler for his expertise and gracious use of his computer in preparing the final printouts; and to Joanne Siegrist for her insight on photo captions. I am especially grateful to my wife, Miriam, for her immersion in the project by reading diaries and letters and helping me match photographs with other data, but especially for her patience and long suffering with piles of photos, papers, and memorabilia on every flat surface in the house.

• I also wish to express appreciation to the many persons whose photographs enhance and illustrate my story. My special thanks go to Jay Whitwill, Jackson Young, Paul Miller Jr. and Frank Brooks. I regret that there are others I have missed thanking for a wide variety of reasons: Time has a way of severing relationships, whereabouts and even existence. To everyone who has shared in this book I am grateful.

• I am indebted to John F. Smith, curator of the Shamokin Fire Museum, Shamokin, Pennsylvania. Mr. Smith was very gracious in sharing details with me of the great Shamokin Fire of 1916 in which my mother lost everything. He even provided a list of burned out tenants which included my mother's name.

Printed by
MODERN PRINTING & GRAPHICS
Sarasota, Florida

WHERE DO ALL THE MEMORIES GO?

My Life Story
And Extended Family Influences

1921 – 1997

To Le Roy & Irene Bechler in gratitude for many fine memories.

Lowell

D. LOWELL NISSLEY

Published by

Nüssli Haus

Sarasota, FL

NISSLEY COAT OF ARMS, 1628

Author's Note

I WONDER ABOUT THE FEELINGS OF WAR ORPHANS, adopted, abandoned, or otherwise forebear-less people. No one ever asked me if I wanted to be born in Lemoyne, Pennsylvania with genes from Switzerland, France, Ireland, Italy, and England; and yet here I am, and the knowledge of where I came from helps me know who I am, giving some sense of where I am and where I may go. To be void of history I should think would make one lonely and reinforce insecurity. In poring over photographs - some 140 years old - comparing physical features and facial expressions in the painstaking process of identification, reading diaries and personal letters over 100 years old, does something to one's psyche. After awhile I realize this is me. I am grateful for my ancestry, warts and all, for the Christian Faith of my ancestors, even though it may have been defined by different definitions than today's expectations of faith.

I submit this as a contribution to my history and to those who share this common heritage. For others who may read this, they may not, nor in fact cannot read through my glasses. Hopefully it will generate images, feelings, and new discovery of one's own genre.

Memories are one thing which can be taken when one leaves this world and a U-Haul will not be needed. My imprint on the world will fade along with me except for a very short period in the lives of those closest to me, and in time they too will go. Was it Shakespeare's Macbeth who said, "Life's but a walking shadow. ... It is a tale told by an idiot, full of sound and fury, signifying nothing"? I'm glad life need not be so cynical even though I know that in the vast scheme of things my life and that of my family will become diluted in the great sea of history to the point of total insignificance. But it is today that is important. Yesterday is gone - never to return. Tomorrow never comes. it's true, I am vulnerable to romanticizing yesterday and not everything yesterday was sweet and lovely. I am reminded of the woman who said to one of the editors of the English magazine, "Punch", "Your magazine is not as good as it used to be". To which the editor replied, "Madam, it never was". The best I can do with my memories of yesterday is to build upon them for greater tomorrows. Only today is mine to enjoy and to fashion memories for yesterdays. What future generations do with my todays is not mine to say. Today at least I still have my memories while I'm creating new ones.

Believe it or not, I can remember events when I was two years old, so why then do I have trouble remembering the name of a certain street I travel often, or the flowering vine so fragrant in our back yard? Does my brain have a dust bin for discarded memories? Who decides what gets thrown away? On the other hand, what's going on that one can remember anything at all? How is it that a ball player can chase a fly ball calculating the speed and direction while he runs arriving at the right spot at the right time to catch it? God's marvelous creation of the mind is truly a wondrous thing. For example, have you ever thought about motorists on a six-lane highway each constantly calculating his/her speed, the speed of drivers behind, before and alongside, all the while concentrating on the daily expectations of job, play, shopping, politics or what-have-you and its been noted that some can even put on makeup, shave, read a book or talk on the phone. Is the brain a glorified computer of Divine manufacture? Does maintaining a good relationship with the manufacturer guarantee better service?

D. Lowell Nissley
June 1997
Sarasota, Florida

AN EARLY 20TH CENTURY THRESHING RIG, *circa 1908*
FRONT COVER:

This is a photograph taken by my father at the Nissley family homestead in Manor Township, Lancaster, Pennsylvania, owned and operated by Jonas L. Nissley, my grandfather. The farm is located along Miller Road, near Millersville, Pennsylvania. The threshing equipment belonged to John C. Nissley, my father's brother. John C. Nissley is sitting in his 1907 Studebaker. In 1994 I took a photo from almost the same spot in the field. It shows little change. The windmill is gone and the hedge is gone but the barn, house and tobacco barn look very much like they did ninety years ago.

*Table
of
Contents*

Memories of Childhood *2*

    Valley Forge, Pennsylvania
    Lemoyne, Pennsylvania
    Lionville, Pennsylvania
    Frank C. Nissley
    John M. Madden
    Mary Jessica Madden Miller Nissley
    Shamokin Hotel Fire
    Naomi Charles Nissley
    Black Horse Hill
    Christmases
    Cousins
    Tampa, Florida
    Ida Street Mennonite Church
    Eastern Mennonite School

Portfolio of Nissley Photographs *74*

Memories Beyond Childhood *84*

    Civilian Public Service
    Cedar Rapids Victory
    Eastern Mennonite University
    The Brackbill Family

Memories of Christian Service *98*

    Crystal Springs, Kansas
    Jay Whitwill
    Kansas City, Kansas
    Goshen, Indiana

Memories of the Southeast Mennonite Conference *109*

Memories Updated *110*

Nissley/DuBois Family Time Lines *115-116*

Memories Revisited *119*

Author's Afterthoughts *122-123*

Index *124-127*

VALLEY FORGE HOUSE, *1923*

This was our home at Valley Forge, Pennsylvania along Valley Road when I was two years old. We lived here from 1923 to 1925. I am standing in front of the house by a large tree.

Memories Of Childhood

My OLDEST MEMORIES go back to Valley Forge, Pennsylvania where my family lived when I was two years old. They moved there from Lemoyne, Pennsylvania where I was born and I remember a lot of things about Valley Forge. People say, "You just remember what you've heard people say," but while I'm sure there is truth here, much of what I remember is too personal and insignificant for adults to talk about. I remember the gooseberry patch along the fence by the road, sliding down the outside cellar doors with my sister, and being upset with a cousin who was pulling my wagon around the porch upside down and abusing my pedal car. I also remember the porch that ran three quarters of the way around the house. It was a great place to play. Unfortunately, we don't have porches anymore. In former days people would sit on a swing in the evening or just on the stoop visiting with neighbors and passersby. Today we have air conditioning so we go inside, shut the door, all the windows, and watch TV. The porch has been enclosed with double pane windows, carpeted and double locks installed on the doors.

I remember when my sister, Naomi, (18 months older) put her hand on the red-hot potbellied stove in the living room, and my aunt and my mother rushed to scrape raw potato to put on the burn. I also remember looking at the glow in the sky when the neighbor's barn burned.

When I was four, my father went back to his roots, when he bought a small farm near Lionville, Pennsylvania. He realized that being an itinerant photographer was not in the best interests of a family with two small children. On the farm he raised chickens for a butter & egg route on the Main Line near Philadelphia.

My father was the fourth of eight children born to Jonas & Fanny (Charles) Nissley on the Nissley homestead near Washington Boro in Lancaster, Pennsylvania. He was born June 23, 1882 and left home at twenty-one to take up photography. He was among the sixth generation of Nissleys in this country coming from Zurich, Switzerland in 1717. After he left home he never

FRANK C. NISSLEY, *about 1898*

went back except for short visits, so I never knew my Lancaster cousins very well, except Verna and Frances Miller who lived on the old Nissley Homestead. Their mother was my father's sister, Emma, and our occasional visits would be at their home. I remember the double swing in the yard where we would all play, and the concord grape vines along the porch and down the outside stairway. There was a narrow, winding stairway from the kitchen to the upstairs where my eighty-year-old grandmother died when she fell down those stairs in 1930. The homestead is no longer in the family, and I visited there in 1994. The grapevine is gone and an odd looking garage has been added. But when I walked down the lane towards the fields, past the old tobacco barn, all the old smells came back to me. I guess tobacco smells don't change much.

NISSLEY FAMILY PROTRAIT, *1886*
To my knowledge this is the oldest known photograph of my father's family, probably taken in a studio.

Front row l-r: Franklin, my father (b 1882), Samuel (b 1886), Susan (b 1879) Emma was born in 1891 after this photo was taken.

Back row: Father Jonas (b 1845), Amos (b 1875), Mother Fanny (b 1848), John (b 1877)

NISSLEY FAMILY PORTRAIT, *about 1917*
This photo was taken at the Nissley homestead.

Front row l-r: Emma, Father Jonas L. Nissley, Mother Fanny H. Charles Nissley, Susan.

Back row: Frank, (my father), John, Sam, Amos.

EXTENDED NISSLEY FAMILY PORTRAIT, *1919*
My father's parents are in the middle of the front row. Jonas holds his cane while his wife simply sits by his side. My father and mother are in the back holding my sister, Naomi. My father wears a flashy white neck scarf that sweeps to the left.

FRANCES KENDIG NISSLEY, *about 1960*
Frances Kendig was the wife of Samuel C. Nissley
my father's younger brother.

ABRAM K. McDONALD, *about 1960*
Abram K. McDonald was the husband of Susan Nissley,
my father's older sister.

FRANK, A ROCKER and HIS PAPER, *about 1960*
This photo was taken at the home of his daughter
Naomi Limont, in Germantown, Pennyslvania.

A GARDENER FOREVER, *about 1970*
My father grew fantastic vegetables on the horse
farm near Phoenixville, Pennsylvania where he lived
after my mother's death in 1963. He would display
them for sale along the road.

***COUNTRY SCHOOL PORTRAIT**, about 1893*
This is the elementary school near Washington Boro where my father went to school.
He is in the first row, the third from the left. Teacher: John Drum.

ENGINE TROUBLE?, *1923*
This was my very first car. My fascination with cars came early. I wear a typical toddler's dress for little boys.

COLLEGEVILLE HOUSE, *1919*
This is 339 East Ninth Avenue, Collegeville, Pennsylvania where my parents lived when my sister, Naomi, was born in 1919. The car is my mother's Saxon.

LEMOYNE HOUSE, *1921*
This is 100 Walnut Street, Lemoyne, Pennsylvania where I was born in 1921. Note my
father's 1916 Pullman car.

HARRISBURG FROM LEMOYNE, *about 1921*
This is Harrisburg, Pennsylvania from our back yard at Lemoyne looking across
the Susquehanna River.

9

LIONVILLE HOUSE, *1994*
This is where we lived in Lionville, Pennsylvania. when my father traded photography for raising chickens in 1925.

"DOWN TOWN" LIONVILLE, *1925*
Today Lionville is only a hesitation along Route #100 on the way to the Pennsylvania Turnpike, near Downingtown, Pennsylvania.

NISSLEY HOMESTEAD, *1994*
This is where my father grew up near Washington Boro, Pennsylvania.
The house and barn were built by Samuel E. Nissley, my Great Grandfather.
The barn was built in 1857 and the house in 1860.

A LITTLE GIANT IN NEBRASKA MUD, *1915*
In Omaha my father installed a schooner body from the Johnson Danforth Company.
Note the tire chains on the solid rubber tires.

My father specialized in child photography, going from door to door photographing them in their homes or outside if the weather was good. He had "Callers Out" who would make the initial sales contact with the child's mother. If the response was favorable, a chalk mark was made on the sidewalk to signal my father coming along maybe 30 minutes later allowing time to wash and dress the children. After a few days he would return with proofs from which the family would place their order. On some occasions he would rent the local theater and show the children's pictures on the screen before taking orders. In the early 1900's it was a big deal to see your children's picture on the screen. My mother became one of his "Callers Out."

In 1915 he bought a Little Giant truck, outfitted it with a closed body and xylophone, and drove it to the San Francisco World's Fair, plying his trade along the way. I have his personal 1915 diary.

FRANK C. NISSLEY, "BUSINESS MAN"
about 1905

A MOBILE PHOTO STUDIO, *1915*
This is my father's photography crew and the Little Giant Truck he drove to the San Francisco World's Fair in 1915. My father is at the wheel.

MARY MCCLOSKEY, (1771-1860), *1857*
She was my Great Great Grandmother from Ireland. She was born in Dublin, Ireland in 1771 and died in Philadelphia, Pennyslvania in 1860. In Ireland she and her family were of the Catholic faith but she became a Methodist after coming to the United States. She was my grandfather's grandmother.

SAMPLER, *Late 1700's*
This sampler was made in Ireland by my Great, Great, Grandmother, Mary Ann McCloskey. She likely made this sampler as a young school girl anticipating marriage.

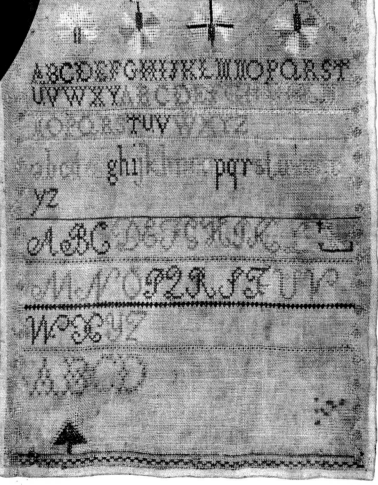

At the beginning of the 19th century there was a baby named John Madden born in New York, who - when he grew up - became a marble inspector traveling between England and America. In Philadelphia he married Mary Ann Morrow after which they moved to Seven Points, New York, and on June 7, 1828, while John was on a business trip to England, their first baby was born. The nurse - a devoted Catholic - sneaked the baby out of the house to a local priest to have it baptized. The priest christened him "John Azra" (John later substituted "Morrow" for "Azra", signing his name "John M. Madden"). Shortly after this the baby's mother received word, along with some personal effects, that her husband had drowned in the English Channel. Then Mary with baby John moved back to Philadelphia to live with her mother, where she later met and married Alonzo George Washington Dewey and they had two sons, William and Jim, and a daughter, Ruth. When John Jr. was fourteen, he was indentured to a brush maker, working in a brush factory and delivering brushes. One of his regular deliveries was to an invalid woman who seemed to take special interest in him as though she knew him. She would arrange frequent visits but would never allow him or her husband to meet. John learned later that this woman's husband was actually his father, John Madden Sr. and that he had not drowned in the English Channel after all. Details of the event are no longer known, but when he returned and learned of his wife's remarriage he - for some unknown reason - never revealed himself but instead also remarried. Another scenario may have been that the drowning was staged and his disappearance may actually have been abandonment, but we will never know.

"ORPHAN" MARY MADDEN, 1863

The initial introduction of my grandfather to the orphan Mary is not known. But in 1858 he was thirty, single and living at home. He had already developed an affection for the eight-year-old (circa) and actually executed an adoption giving her the name "Madden". It also began a long relationship not without conflict. We know little about Mary's history except that her mother was still alive even though Mary was in a Philadelphia orphanage. Mary became a source of great joy but also pain and disappointment. According to his 1858 diary there was opposition to his having Mary and this was very upsetting to him. On a diary entry dated February 26, 1858 he said, "I have since learned that it was the Wynkoops that told Mary's mother where we lived and turned treacherous to me and mother. It will never be forgotten". Another time he threatened to move "... away off to Kansas or Nebraska. Then I will be free from all my enemies. [Kansas] wild woods, wild river, wild lakes, wild birds, wild winds, wild flowers, wild insects, wild wilderness in far west".

Years later while in the Union Army during the Civil War he sent money to Mary and in a December 31, 1864 response from Savannah, Georgia to a November 29 letter from Mary, he said "... I had no idea you were so angry with me for I do assure you I will never intrude my disagreeable presence upon you again. ... what has possessed your mother to act as you said she did? ... why would she make you so much trouble? ... I am very sorry that you have completely turned against me. ... I have been anxious to get home but now I care very little when or whether I ever come home. ... I had no idea that I was so hated and detested".

It would be good to know what finally happened to Mary. We do know that some years later she married my grandfather's half-brother, Joseph, but was then divorced on September 16, 1873. My grandfather did come home after the war and in 1871 married Josephine Bogia the girl next door who fifty years later became my grandmother. What finally happened to Mary? We don't know, but for a brief spell we could pull the curtain aside to witness some mid-eighteenth century drama in the life of my grandfather.

When the Civil War broke out both John Madden Sr. and John Madden Jr., along with the Dewey step-brothers, all joined the Union Forces. One day during the engagement of the Confederate and Union Forces at Gettysburg, Pennsylvania there was a providential meeting of a father and son for the first time - John Madden Sr. met John Madden Jr. face to face. "Is this my son John?" he asked. John Sr. was now a Captain in the Cavalry and had to leave but said, "I'll see you again," but never did because his unit was captured shortly after and he died of cholera in Libby Prison, Richmond, Virginia. Libby Prison, a tobacco ware-house, was used for the incarceration of Union Officers. It was among the most notorious in the Confederacy with thousands dying there of neglect and disease.

Following the war John Jr. was stationed in Washington, DC where he served as a guard at the White House and once met President Lincoln. After his discharge he moved to Philadelphia to live with his mother, where on July 10, 1871 he married the sixteen-year-old girl next door, Mary Josephine Bogia. The two John Maddens were my Grandfather and Great Grandfather, and Mary Bogia was my Grandmother.

MAIL AND NEWSPAPERS AT "A. OF P." HEADQUARTERS

JOHN M. MADDEN (1828-1906), about 1864
This photo was taken during the Civil War. John M Madden stands under the arrow. As a young child he never knew his father. About the time of his birth it was thought that he drowned in the English Channel. John grew up as a stepbrother to William and James Dewey after his mother married Alonzo George Washington Dewey. It later turned out that his father had not drowned and they met each other for the first time during the war where they were both enlisted in the Union Army.

John M. Madden, my grandfather, was a volunteer in the Union Forces of the Civil War in the same unit with his stepfather, Alonzo George Washington Dewey, his half-brother, Joseph Madden, and his two half brothers James, and William. It seems unusual for a soldier to keep a detailed account of events in the midst of the horrors of war but my grandfather did just that. The following are a few excerpts from his 1864 diary.

A January 1, 1864 entry places him in Company A, 109th. Pennsylvania Volunteer Veterans in Bridgeport, Alabama - the northeast corner of the State not far from Chattanooga, Tennessee:

"... I was almost frozen to death in the night. The tent blew over last night. I never suffered such cold in my life. Awful hurricane blowing down, northwest, wrought down off the Tennessee River. I sat on end of the bed and held my socks under my arms to thaw them. My pants are frozen stiff. I ran in my stocking feet, down, down to the shanty where all the guards are, to thaw my pants. My hair, full of white frost. ... Cold, cold winter night."

My grandfather was a sensitive man enjoying music, art and books many of which he took along to war. He had eyes and ears for things not obvious to most people, like birds and crickets singing. His assignment was to assist the medical team, cook for the doctors and help with surgery. In Indianapolis he wrote:

"... from peas to beans. The doctors got ham. Crickets and insects, all night singing in the trees."

By the middle of May they had moved further south into Tennessee and Georgia, engaging the Rebel forces.

May 14 to May 21, 1864

"... Battle all day for three days. ... I made coffee and fried ham, then fixed potatoes for Doctor Dunn's breakfast. ... We were stopped by Rebel shells flying overhead. One dropped in the mud near me. ... Doctor used his instrument to take off a left-hand finger. I cleaned the knife by wiping. Very many dead horses along the roads. The hills are covered with dead Rebels. ... A long line of Cavalry passed by. ... Doctor's got ham. ... Crickets and insects, all night singing in the trees. ... hot sun, and fast marching. We passed Rebel group and some wounded men of ours. The men plundered all the houses. ... I fried his [Dr. Dunn] ham and three eggs. ... cannon roaring all day. I fell into a stream - lost butcher knife. ... I awoke laying by Dr. Dunn. ... Meadow Larks and other birds singing.

... got Doctor's supper, ham and corn cakes, beautiful golden sunset. All the camp looking at it. ... passed Rebel smallpox hospital - all burned. ... washed Doctor's towel in muddy stream. ... We beat retreat for the first time in a week."

May 22 to May 27, 1864

"... rested in camp in Cassville [Georgia] all day. ... cleaned all the amputation instruments up. ... Whippoorwills in all directions ... beautiful sunset in the West. —We crossed the Altoona Mountains. ... I threw away some books. —heavy skirmish. Many wounded. ... battle raging. ... rained most all night. ... Doctor called me to go clean instruments. ... amputating continually. ... I felt sick all day the bowels and dispepsia. ... Dunn burning, amputating all afternoon. Crickets. Night Hawks, cannon and brass band all going. Bowels are troublesome. ... bullets whistling all around and over us. Death on every side. ... A terrible attack on our breastworks and were driven back with great loss. Intensely hot! Cannon and musket fire all day."

May 28 to June 22, 1864

"... Sargent Story of Co S brought in wounded. His right leg taken off below the knee. ... Starry - light moon shining. ... The Rebels made an assault in force on our breastworks twice, and were driven back. ... We have strong hopes of the war ending this Summer [1864]. ... We passed General Sherman on the road. ... when will the war end? There are about 20 of the 100 gone. I hope and believe it will end this year. ... Battle all day. ... got supper in the dark. ... Steward stepped into my frying pan and upset my bacon. ... Skirmishes firing all night long. ... Crickets and other insects singing. ... A Blackbird singing most sweetly. —A partridge whistling. ... terrible cannonading all night. ... drizzle, rain, mud. All my things are mouldy and my books mildewed. Cannon roaring all afternoon. One continuous roar. Selfridge is shot through the hips."

June 26 to July 3, 1864

"... Rebels quiet for Sunday. ... We shelled out of hospital! Intolerably hot these last three days. ... Rebels shelled hospital. One struck near me at breastworks. ... Flies are awful! ... Intensely hot! Flies here are worse. The blood on the tent is the cause of it. ... My poison ivy is awful. Birds all singing. ... We moved along the Atlanta Turnpike. ... Trees literally torn to pieces, with shot and shells. Shanties all riddled. One conical shell stuck half way through a tree."

July 4 to July 21, 1864

"When will the war end? … A fine view of Atlanta - we all looked at it on a hill. Ten miles from Atlanta. … We took 300 Rebel prisoners. … We all think the war is most ended. … Musical blackbirds in the woods. … When will the war end and we can go home? Peace, liberty, and independence. … Locust singing lately, in the trees. … Rebels all gone again. … The pit [latrine] and dead horse intolerable! Flies awful! Made soup. … I baked a plum pie, for Dr. Dunn, and a shortcake. … Whippoor-wills singing in the hollow. … We moved seven or eight mile across the Chatahoochee River. … I made coffee of muddy water. … I feel sick, and dispectic. … We passed along a ridge from which we could see a glimpse of Atlanta. … Dr. took a bath in the brook. … There was a dead horse in the creek. … Coleman killed. Captain Elliot killed. … Flies are awful! … Heavy shelling commenced again! Dr. had the crutches cut and the operating table made ready. … Stretchers bringing in our wounded and dying. Dr. Dunn operating. Shelling heavy! … Long lines of dead and dying lying around us!"

July 22 to July 28, 1864

"… All moved up to toward Atlanta. … Cannonading and shelling Atlanta, all day. … Flies never worse! They're in droves and clouds. … We marched two or three miles further, from near Chatahoochee onto the hill for a better position for shelling Atlanta. One continual cannonading all night, as well as all day. The air is a body of dust, sulphurous smoke, and dead mules. No birds, no insects, except for those classed as vermine. … Terrible cannonading, all day, all night. I and Tom Taylor went on a hill to see Atlanta burn at night. … cannonading continually - fires in Atlanta. … I baked Dr. a rice pudding. I and Taylor and Jim took glasses over the hill to see fires in Atlanta.."

Near the end of this journal his notations become less and more brief accompanied with sketches of Atlanta, birds, flowers and trees. From the 75th day (July 30), to the 100th. day the pages are blank, except for one line on day 97 in August:

"Is the war ended yet?"

It's not known if he kept further diaries during the war or not. We do know he was in Savannah, Georgia in December of 1864 because of a letter he wrote to "Orphan Mary" (see page 14).

JOSEPH MADDEN, early 1860's

Joseph was the half-brother of my Grandfather, John M. Madden. After my Great-Grandfather, John Madden, was thought to have drowned in the English Channel in 1828, his "widow", Mary Ann Morrow, had a serious romance with a man named "Sixty". Sixty's parents so objected to this relationship they had him sent off to South America where he became ill and died before he and Mary Ann could get married. Joseph then was born the result of this relationship. Mary Ann later married Alonzo George Washington Dewey and Joseph grew up in this family taking the name Madden after his mother's first marriage. We know that Joseph lived for a time in South Dakota and was mustered out of the 40th Indiana Regiment in the Union forces of the Civil War in Lafayette, Indiana and then lived in Romney, Indiana. His second wife was "orphan" Mary Madden, the adopted child of my grandfather, John M. Madden. This marriage ended in divorce September 16, 1873. Seven weeks later on November 2 Joseph Madden married Sarah Jane Jackson. I have no further knowledge of Joseph except that he had a daughter, Emily, who lived in Atlanta, Georgia. Joseph was my grandmother's half brother-in-law.

MARY JOSEPHINE BOGIA MADDEN (1855-1924), *around 1920*

My grandmother, Mary Josephine Bogia Madden, lived in Philadelphia, Pennyslvania next door to Mary Morrow Madden Dewey, mother of John M. Madden. She was only sixteen when John M. Madden came home from the Civil War. They were married July 10, 1871 and had five children: Ruth, Joseph, John (Jack), Jessica (my mother), and Alyce Ione.

EXTENDED MADDEN FAMILY PORTRAIT, *1923*

This photo was taken at our home in Valley Forge, Pennyslvania.
Top row: Frank Boyer, George Tripler, Charles Boyer, Jr., Charles Boyer, Sr.,
Joseph Madden, Sr.

Front row l-r: Fred Boyer, John Boyer, Jospeh Madden, Jr., (sitting), Alice Edna Boyer (holding
Dorothy Tripler), Retta Madden, Jr., (holding Naomi Nissley), Ione Smiley (holding Audrey
Ellison), Ruth Boyer, Jr., Eugene Boyer, Lowell Nissley (in the car).

Middle row: John A. Madden (Jack), Frank Smiley, Reba Boyer Ellison, Gertrude "Gertie"
Madden, Retta Madden, Sr., Mary J. Bogia Madden, Agnes Boyer, Ruth Madden Boyer,
Alyce Ione Madden Smiley, Frank Nissley.

MADDEN FAMILY PORTRAIT, *about 1920*
My mother stands with her sibblings and her mother. l-r: Alyce Ione,
Mary Jessica (my mother), Joseph, John A., Ruth, Mary J. Madden (my grandmother).

My mother was born in Philadelphia, also in 1882, of Irish, British, Italian and French extraction. While my father identified with Miller, Herr, Charles and Lehman, my mother's family names were Madden, Bogia, Boyer, Smiley and DuBois. Her father fought in the Civil War as a Union soldier and met his father for the first time in the Army.

My mother, the fourth of five children, was born when her father was fifty-four years old. He died April 17, 1906, at the age of seventy-eight, and my grandmother August 5, 1924, at the age of sixty-five. I have some memories of my grandmother as a tall dignified woman when she lived with my Aunt Ona Smiley in Malvern, Pennsylvania.

HAUNTED HOUSE, 1970

This house is located on Conestoga Road, formerly the Lincoln Highway, at Dales Ford, Pennsylvania, about 18 miles west of Philadelphia, Pennyslvania. The haunted house story is told by my mother who lived at this house with her family when she was 16 years old. She tells about blood stains on bedroom floors and at least one bedroom door which could not be made to stay shut at night even when propped shut. At times family members would hear a crash in the kitchen as though all the pots and pans had fallen to the floor but upon investigation everything was in perfect order.

According to my mother, growing up was hard. Her father was thirty-three years her mother's senior and in later years found it difficult to provide for a family of seven. In those days there was nothing akin to Social Security and families were left to their own ingenuity and sharing of friends and neighbors. This was during the time of the 1866-1914 economic hard times following the Civil War which I am told was equal to the 1930's experience. Life was mostly a survival existence with few pleasures and those being derived in large measure from the intimacies of a close family. I have a few pages of an 1883 diary of my grandfather's in which he describes his job as a school janitor in Philadelphia where he often spent the night in the damp cellar to keep the fires going. My mother was less than a year old and at this time the family lived fifteen miles away in the Berwyn area, so my grandfather often did not get home even on weekends. Some diary pages from my mother's oldest sister, Ruth, reveal some of the hardships in those days. She tells of caring for my mother when she had diphtheria and almost died in 1889. My mother was seven years old and Aunt Ruth was eighteen. She tells of the time she received 49¢ for the sale of some eggs and walked to the doctor's office in Malvern to pay for some medicine for my mother. And, by the way, the doctor made house calls, stopping in most every day.

When my mother was 16 she lived with her family in the "haunted house" in Dales Ford, Pennsylvania. Her story goes back to the late 1700s, when the house was the well known Blue Ball Inn. At the time it was owned and operated by a woman named Prissy Robinson. From 1799 to 1831, she would murder travelling salesmen for their wares and money burying them in the dirt floor of the cellar. Oral history says she killed her husband by asking him to help her bring a barrel of wine up from the cellar. When part way up she let go and he was crushed by the barrel. Once while my mother's family lived at this house, a man stopped and told his personal experience. At the time he said he was a jewelry salesman. One night he awoke at the sound of voices. It was Prissy and her husband planning how they would kill him. His room was on the ground floor so he fled through the window. He suddenly remembered his jewelry under his pillow. He went back to retrieve it and then escaped through the

MY MOTHER, A TEENAGER, *about 1898*
Mary Jessica Madden

orchard. Over the years numerous articles have been written in Philadelphia newspapers about Prissy. It is said that when she died in 1831, she cursed saying, "They'll never find my money", turned her face to the wall and died. Many believe she is still in the old house. There are other stories like her constant fight with the Pennsylvania Railroad for killing one of her cows, and the apparition my grandmother saw once in an upstairs back bedroom while scrubbing the floor ---- but that's for another time - perhaps at Halloween. Giving credence to some of these stories has been the unearthing of human skeletons under the dirt floor of the kitchen and in the cellar during subsequent remodeling.

HARRY S. MILLER,
about 1895
My mother's first
husband (1872-1907).
He lived in Glen Moore,
Pennsylvania.

MY MOTHER, *1908*
This photo was taken
just one year after her
first husband, Harry
Miller, died from
Tuberculosis. She too
was diagnosed with
terminal TB in 1907.

In 1904 at age twenty-two, my mother married Harry Miller, aged thirty-one, a widower with two children, Grace and Charles. They were married January 14, 1904, and in the next three years had three children of their own, Ruth, Henry Rutter, and Paul. When Harry died April 4, 1907 of tuberculosis, my mother was left with five small children and was herself diagnosed with terminal tuberculosis. What are the options for a young widow with no home, no job and terminally ill? She decided to take a shot at curing herself by getting a job that would keep her outdoors and active. Before going into business for herself, she worked six years as a traveling photographer for Will Chronister of York, Pennsylvania.

It's not clear who took care of her two stepchildren, Grace and Charles, but I understand that Charles lived all his life in the Paoli, Pennsylvania area, but few family relationships were ever maintained. I never met him. Of her own children, Henry Rutter died in 1909 at age four and one half and Ruth in 1911 at age five and one half. In both cases my mother was on the road, and in the case of Ruth at least, was working in Florida. I remember the surviving son, Paul, very well. He was fifteen years old when I was born. He grew up in Girard College in Philadelphia. In the years following, he intersected my life on many occasions until his death from cancer in 1964.

MILLER FAMILY PORTRAIT, *1906*
This was my mother's first husband and their family. Harry had three children, Violet, Charles and Grace, from a former marriage. His first wife, Margaret Brown, died Ocober 3, 1901. Ruth, Henry Rutter, and Paul were my mother's children to Harry S. Miller, her first husband.

Front row: Ruth, Grace, Henry Rutter, Charles.

Back row: Father Harry S. Miller, Mother Mary (Madden) Miller holding Paul.

23

GRACE and CHARLES MILLER, *about 1914*
Grace was born 12/19/1900 and Charles 2/11/1899. They were the children of my mother's first husband, Harry Miller by his first wife, Clara Margaret Brown, 1868-1901. Harry died of tuberculosis in 1907. My mother had three children from her marriage to Harry Miller: Ruth, Henry Rutter, and Paul.

BROTHER and SISTER, *1908*
These are my mother's first two children from her first marriage. Henry Rutter Miller (left) and Ruth Miller (right). Henry wears a typical little boys dress; he died in 1909 at age four and a half.

RUTH MILLER IN CASKET, *1911*
Ruth was five and one-half years old.

HENRY RUTTER MILLER IN CASKET, 1909
Henry was four and one-half years old.

MARY JESSICA MADDEN, MY MOTHER,
about 1885

MY MOTHER, *1908*
This photo was taken just one year after her first husband, Harry Miller, died from Tuberculosis.

MY MOTHER IN HER FLORIDA BATHING SUIT,
1911

ALONE", 1911
My mother was in Florida when her daughter, Ruth, died. This photo was taken looking out over the Gulf of Mexico in Tampa just after she received word of her daughter's death.

A SOON-TO-BE-BRIDE, 1918
Mary Jessica Madden the year she married my father.

MY MOTHER, 1950

WILL CHRONISTER, *1913*

Will stands in front of a georgeous palm tree in Tampa, Florida. He was a mutual friend of both my parents. When my mother first took up photography she worked for him for two years.

WILL CHRONISTER
and HIS 1903 RAMBLER, *1903*

SMILEY FAMILY PORTRAIT, *around 1920*
My mother's youngest sister is Alyce Ione. Her only child is Ione and her husband is Frank Smiley. While growing up our family was closer to Uncle Frank & Aunt Ona than any other aunt or uncle.

ELIZABETH ANN NELL CHRONISTER,
1920's
Mrs. Chronister (born September 11, 1851) of York, Pennsylvania, was the mother of Will Chronister (born January 12, 1871), a photographer friend of my parents. Our family would occasionally visit her on weekends and I remember her huge cat. Someone told us kids that it had an operation that made it grow so big. Mrs. Chronister gave our family an antique cuckoo clock and the Chronister family Bible. Today the clock hangs on our living room wall.

RETOUCHING PHOTOS, about 1917
My mother worked for herself until 1916 when she was burned out in the Great Shomokin Hotel Fire. In 1917 she began to work for my father.

On December 15, 1916, my mother was burned out in the most serious fire in the history of Shamokin, Pennsylvania, a fire that threatened for a time to wipe out the entire business section of the town. High winds and biting cold hampered fire-fighters. Eighty families were rendered homeless, fifteen business places and twenty-five buildings were destroyed in the $500,000 fire. The fire began in the basement of the Malarkey Music House in the McWilliams Building and spread rapidly up a ventilation shaft destroying the building in just forty-five minutes. My mother was one of sixty-two tenants in this building. She lost everything except what she wore, including several hundred dollars worth of photographs spread out on the bed, ready for delivery, and a brand new coat hanging behind the door. All she took was her old coat.

She wrote to an acquaintance, Frank Nissley, whom she had met in Pottstown, Pennsylvania and asked for a job - which she got - and thus began a long journey for them and for me. She tells of their engagement: She was sorting photographs when my father came into the room, kissed her and then made a hasty retreat. They were married November 11, 1918. My sister, Naomi, was born in 1919 and I was born in 1921. My mother tells how my father used to smoke cigars, but one day after Naomi was born, he flicked his cigar butt out the car window saying, "That's my last cigar." And it was.

AFTER THE FIRE, *1916*
These photos show part of the rubble in the wake of the worst fire in the history of Shamokin, Pennsylvania.
My mother said she found a small child in a stairway. The two of them were the last to leave the building.

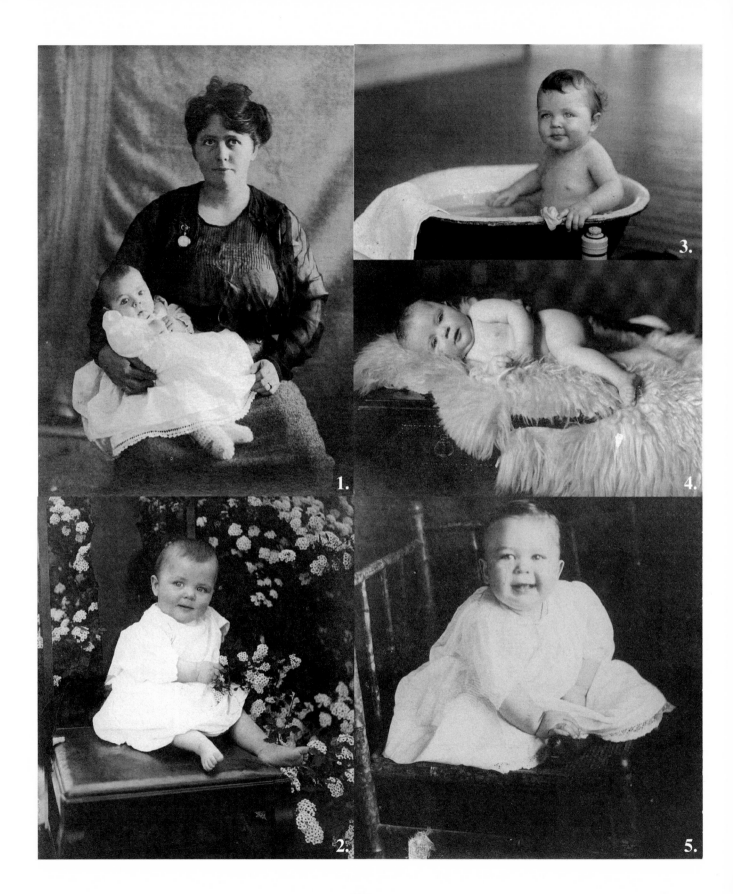

1.

2.

3.

4.

5.

BROTHER and SISTER, *1919-1923*
Here are a few selections from the many pictures taken of my sister and me by our parents:

1. My mother holding me in 1921.

2. Naomi, 1920

3. Naomi, 1919

4. Naomi, 1919

5. Lowell, 1921

6. Naomi, 1923

7. Naomi and Lowell, 1923

8. Naomi and Lowell, 1923

SCHOOL DAZE, *1930*
These are school photos from the
St. Matthews one-room school.

CUPIE DOLL, *1923*
My sister, Naomi won a children's beauty contest
in West Chester, Pennsylvania dressed in this outfit.

THREE SIBLINGS, *1921*
My sister sitting on the table and my half-
brother, Paul, holds me in our home at
Lemoyne, Pennsylvania.

33

WHITE FENCES, *1994*
White Fences is a recent example of the work by my sister, Naomi Limont. It is a water color from one of my Amish farm photos near New Holland, Pennsylvania.

My sister had a natural talent for art, which was first evident when we lived on the farm at Lionville. She was in first grade and would come home with drawings, a prelude to what she later developed into an enviable national reputation. She earned a BFA from the University of Pennsylvania, and a MFA from Tyler School of Art. She traveled in Europe on a scholarship from a William Emlen Cresson Foreign Traveling Scholarship, from the Pennsylvania Academy of Fine Arts, allowing her to study the great collections of Europe. She has had numerous solo and group exhibitions of her work in well known galleries and museums. A color etching of her, "William Penn's Treaty With the Indians," was among several gifts that Pennsylvania Governor Milton Schapp presented to the President of France, Valerie Giscard D'Estang, in commemoration of the 1976 Bicentennial, held in Philadelphia. Her work is represented in the permanent collection of the Philadelphia Museum of Fine Art.

HAPPY ARTIST, *1980*
My sister, Naomi Charles Nissley Limont, in her Germantown Studio in Philadelphia, Pennsylvania.

I do not remember Naomi's first art work at Lionville but it must have made some impression because I remember visiting Mrs. Gunn, our neighbor, who would give me paper on which I would "draw" squiggly lines, explaining with pride their meaning. My mother never liked us to visit the Gunn's because they were Catholics. I was four and five years old when we lived there and have some vivid memories of it. I remember seeing white chickens being blown through the air during a bad storm which killed many of my father's laying hens, and the pain of trying to walk on wheat stubble barefoot behind the barn. I remember the downstairs layout of the house: Inside the front door to the left was the dining room where the radio   sat on a little table just inside the door. In those days radios had a big horn on top for a speaker, and I remember once during a rare party of family and neighbors (it may have been Halloween), some loose corn went down into the horn making loud cracking/popping sounds, little enhancing the sound of a 1920's radio. To the right of the front door was the living room where I can still see my father sitting at his big desk which had belonged to his father. It was a solid cherry slant top desk with three large drawers and many cubby holes with secret compartments, and was made by Jacob Slannbunge on December 19, 1834. I am fortunate to have this desk occupying space in our present bedroom. I remember walking with my father behind the plow pulled by "Kate" and "Jen," his two mules; and I remember saying, "When I grow up I'm going to be a farmer." I remember playing with my sister in the igloo that my father made for us in the snow drift by the fence along the road and I remember the two of us playing in my father's abandoned Model T Ford housecar behind the house - I wish

POTATO HARVEST, 1926
Harvesting potatoes in Lionville was a family affair.
l-r: Lowell, Naomi, "Kate & Jen" - our mules, and my mother.

I had that today! Even by today's standards it was modern, having a telescoping top. I remember the pain when the doctor ripped the tape off my neck where he had smeared some smelly black salve. My sister and I both had our tonsils removed here and that for me stopped the black goo and tape.

We lived on the Lionville farm only two years before moving in 1927 to a twenty-eight acre farm a few miles away on Blackhorse Hill (just off Route #100) where we lived for five years - the longest we ever lived in one place.

Most of my childhood memories come from Blackhorse Hill. They were happy days. We lived one-eighth mile in on a dirt road which ran between route #100 and route #401. We had no electricity or running water, but we did have six rooms and a "path". I remember doing my homework on the dining room table

BLACKHORSE HILL HOUSE, 1928
This was our home 1927-1932 located on a dirt road between Route #100 and Route #401 in Chester County, Pennyslvania. Note the hammock where my Aunt Ona spent most of one summer when ill with undalent fever. Also note the rose bush where the chipping sparrows built their nest using Aunt Ona's hair. To the right of the house is the lilac bush and behind that our quince tree. Further to the right is the tool shop once inhabited by bumble bees.

by kerosene lamp, and I could not believe how bright a single bulb could be in the center of the ceiling when we finally got electricity. I remember the interior of our house very well. We entered the kitchen from the cement porch where the outside hand-operated pump occupied a prominent position and, yes, I do remember breaking ice in the winter to wash my face and standing over the pipeless furnace on cold mornings to get dressed. I can still hear the thump of the wood as my father filled the furnace in the cellar. I remember the noisy gasoline Maytag washing machine and the pet goose which would help my mother with the wash by grabbing the clothes and dashing them up and down in the water. And speaking about pets, there was "Rusty" a Rhode Island Red rooster, several cats, pet guineas, and two dogs, "Sparky" and "Lady" (not at the same time). Sparky was a mongrel shepherd and was shot by hunters from the woods across the field above our house, which incensed my mother because she thought hunters were a cruel and unnecessary breed anyway. Lady was a collie and was the result of my reading every book by Albert Payson Terhune I could find. He was a breeder of collies somewhere in New Jersey and wrote thrilling stories about the adventures of "Lassie" which inspired me to think that someday I myself might be a breeder of collies.

But there were unhappy days on Blackhorse Hill too, such as stepping on nails sticking up out of boards, poison ivy, yellow jackets and bumble bees. Ah yes, bumble bees! I especially remember the shop where my father kept his vise (I still have it) and other tools necessary to operate a small farm and plant a garden.

BLACKHORSE HILL HOUSE, 1994
Most of my childhood memories come from this house. We lived here 1927-1932.

I remember the time I pounded on the metal side of this shop and how the bumble bees poured out attacking me, even getting into my pants! God helps us to remember the good events, but in His grace, lets us forget much of the pain. I remember when I slipped on the gravel playground at school and broke my right elbow as I was about to clear four feet on the high jump. In order to prevent a stiff arm, the doctor would apply a straight splint for a week or so and then, laying my arm flat on the table (these still were the days when doctors made housecalls) would bend my arm up to break loose the adhesions. He would then splint it in an "L" position and the next time bend it straight. I know it hurt terribly and I can recreate the event, but, thankfully, not the pain. I remember the cold winters and walking the two miles with my sister in the snow and rain to and from the one room country school; and in the Spring, filling our lunch boxes with mushrooms from the meadow on our way home. I remember watching my father, with other adult assistants, jack up the Model T Ford to start it by turning the rear wheel. I also remember cracking black walnuts in the Fall on the barn floor just inside the huge door which opened to the south over the barnyard with the warm sun bathing the barn floor, along with the ten-year-old cracking nuts. Black walnuts are still my favorite.

I remember spending hours in the cherry trees along the road across from our house. There were two yellow oxhart cherry trees, a black oxhart and one honey cherry. Here is where I got my initial experience climbing trees which paid off many years later when I was the only one of twenty applicants hired by the C. J. Nolan Tree Expert Company in Newtown Square, Pennsylvania. Well, it seemed like many years later. Actually it was only about ten, but then ten years is a lifetime to a ten-year old. Those cherry trees are now all gone, falling victim to the Japanese Beetles in the late 30's and early 40's. Regarding trees, I remember spending hours with my dog in the woods above the house where Lady would go on safaris chasing rabbits while I sat on a stump listening to the wind in the trees, the songs of crickets and locusts and birds. It was from that vantage point that I could look out across the little valley to the fields of the farm south of us, and while I don't remember ever meeting those people, I do remember the grandeur of their wheat fields flowing in the wind like ocean waves. I remember finding a dime once under a stone on the path that went up through the woods.

Artwork by my sister, Naomi. Featured in the Mennonite Community Cookbook, page 35.

In the house was a kitchen. Of course! But there are important things about this kitchen. I remember the white kitchen cabinet with its flour and sugar bins, the

***LIONVILLE BARN**, 1926*
It was behind this hedge on the right where my father made igloos in the snow banks for us to play in.

old black wood-burning cook stove with a water-back behind which I hid when company came. There was a wood box and a table for preparing meals and washing dishes (we carried the water in from the outside pump). I also remember the large window sill where I sat with my knees pulled up to my chin, immersed in guilt as I heard my mother tell someone that she planned on getting a bicycle for me for Christmas, but it would not happen because I had lied to her. In looking back now it wasn't all that big a deal, but at the time it was really big because things around our house were very important and abuse of them was not taken lightly. The front door was at the other end of the house from the kitchen and straight ahead was the upstairs stairway - the "Wooden Hill" my father always called it - and to the right was the parlor. We never used the parlor much and it was usually kept dark, but just inside the parlor at the foot of the stairs was a victrola. My mother was upstairs and I was playing records, which we children usually did not do by ourselves. The record was slowing down so I began winding the crank handle when the spring broke with a strange kind of "Thunk-a-Bang!" My mother called down, "What did you do?" I said, "Nothing, I didn't do anything." Obviously this was the wrong answer because she accused me of breaking the victrola and then lying about it. I do not ever remember being whipped by my mother as she had more effective ways of punishment like sitting on a chair for an hour or denying something I wanted - like a bicycle.

I remember our weekly shopping trips to Downington for groceries, clothing, hair cuts, or to visit Dr. Lenhart, the chiropractor. I also remember standing on the front seat of the car operating the windshield wiper for my father to clear the snow.

I remember that my father once used an earthy four-letter word while our family was riding in the car. My mother immediately explained that he was just copying the vulgar language of the men at the dairy where he worked. My, how times have changed. Some of those words today, while maybe not used in church on a Sunday morning, are used in regular conversation by other than vulgar people. For us, however, even though we were not a religious bunch, my mother did insist on some high standards of conduct so that there was never foul language, smoking or drinking in our house.

The chicken & egg business didn't go very well, so my father stopped raising chickens and became a herdsman at Fellowship Farms, a large dairy operation near by, which processed milk for delivery on the Main Line. It was owned by a "Gentleman Farmer" named Dr. Branson. The resident manager was named Hepburn, whose children went to the same one-room school where we went. I remember David Hepburn and a brother who my sister and I thought were snooty and spoiled, which they probably were. We would make trips across the fields to the dump where the Hepburns discarded their junk, and would come home with some fine trophies of discarded Hepburn toys and collectibles - one kid's junk is another kid's treasure. It was like a free flea market and in fact I still have a few iron toy cars and tractors scavenged from that dump. My best friend was Newt Evans who lived on a farm along route #401 on our way to school. His father had a brand new Willys Knight sedan.

This one-room school, St. Matthew's, with Miss McAfee and later Miss Urner, played a crucial part in my educational journey. I started first grade in Haines City, Florida (50 years later I felt proud at being able to drive right to it. The playground was still there but the building was now administrative offices) where my father and Uncle Frank Smiley picked oranges for the Blue Goose Company. Before the school year was up we moved to Desoto Park in Tampa where I finished the year and passed on to the second grade. The next year (1928), school had already been in session several

ST. MATTHEWS SCHOOL*, 1995*
This is the one-room country school where I attended grades 3-6. Our organ came from this school.

weeks when we returned to Florida and I went to two different schools. At the end of the year I did not just fail second grade, but was put back into first grade. I still remember the Spanish architecture of that school with its yellow arches. The next spring (1929) we left Florida before school was out and I was transferred to a one-room country school at Ludwig's Corner on Route #100 to finish the year. Believe it or not, I failed first grade, not even able to figure out the first table - 1x1=1 - but I did enjoy making airplanes from modeling clay. The next fall I should have been in third grade but was still in first so my mother took my sister and me to St. Matthew's, a one-room school two miles in the other direction on Route #401. Here she explained my predicament to Miss McAfee who suggested we try the third grade and see what happens - the rest, as they say, is history. The school had eight grades with a student population of thirty-two. When I was in the sixth grade there were only two of us - Gertrude Twadell and me.

The musical instrument in this school was a Packard foot-operated parlor organ with mirrors and lots of gingerbread, drawers and cubby holes. It was made in Fort Wayne, Indiana. When the School Board wanted to modernize and replace it with a piano, my Aunt Ruth bought it for $15.00. After her death I bought it from her family for $50.00 and it now occupies an important spot on an inside wall of our living room, occasionally filling the house with beautiful music and memories.

On a different note, I remember when my brother, Paul, tried to scare crows in the orchard by firing a 22 caliber pistol from the upstairs bedroom window. He said he didn't know why he held his finger in front of the barrel while he pulled the trigger. My mother drove him to the doctor's office in Downingtown, and it's the only time I remember seeing my mother drive a car. But of course she must have driven more often than that because she drove her own car before her marriage to my father. She would make our sides ache laughing about the time she hit a man with her 1918 Saxon going up Malvern Hill, which was steep even by today's standards. He was sprawled over the front fender all the way to the top, because she did not want to stop before reaching the summit. He crawled off and was no worse for the wear and tear. Today there would have been two ambulances and six lawyers at the scene. I remember the used 1927 Dodge she bought in West Chester. It had a heater on the floor in the back seat - a register over the muffler which you could open to warm your feet. In retaliation my father went to Pottstown and bought a new Model A Ford coupe. I don't know whatever happened to the Dodge but the Ford found its way to Florida with us in it. One event comes to mind: my folks lost heavily at the Downingtown Bank in the crash of 1929, and the Fellowship Farms laid off many of its employees, so my parents sold the farm and bought a house in Tampa, Florida (4112 N. 15th. St.) in 1932, but still returned to Pennsylvania in the summers because work was more plentiful there. In 1933 we bought a housetrailer and were on our way north for the summer with my father trying to revive his photographic skills for travel money along the way, but times had changed and also the photography business had

READY TO ROLL, *1918*
My mother stands beside her 1918 Saxon car and wears a long black coat. Helen Boyer Tripler, a niece and the mother of Dorothy & Constance, is with her.

ARTHUR GUY FARM, 1930's
Near Malvern, Pennsylvania. Formerly this was the Schofield Farm where my wife, Miriam
(Brackbill) was born in 1921. Her father, Milton Brackbill, was farm manager. Sixteen years
later my father was the farm manager and my family moved on the farm. Small world!

changed. With the advent of the Brownie box camera, improved photo technology and my father's ten-year intermission all combined with the "Great Depression" to make photography for him now a no-gainer.

Living with us those days was Ward Holloway, a young man about my sister's age, whose father was a Pentecostal preacher and for some reason was separated from his wife, so my mother offered to have Ward live with us for awhile. Anyway, as we were approaching the outskirts of Perry, Florida, my father, mother and sister were riding up front in the Model A Ford with Ward and me in the housetrailer. The two lane road ran parallel to the railroad for a couple miles and my father, looking for a place to park, didn't notice that the RR tracks crossed the road ahead of him and that a train was coming behind him. Ward and I saw the train coming and that my father was not going to stop. We screamed and yelled but to no avail. The train was an old wood-burning passenger train, blowing its whistle full blast, the engineer seemingly trying to beat us to the crossing. At the last moment, my father, seeing what was happening, hit the brakes while at the same time cutting the wheels hard right and, as the train sped by, the steps on each car tapped the corner of the front bumper, "Clunk," "Clunk," "Clunk," "Clunk." While

I'm this close to Ward Holloway, there is one other thing of import should be said of him. I remember the day he and I were climbing in the great live oaks in the lot behind our house in Tampa. Now we knew by experience that live oak trees are very tough and even small branches would carry a lot of weight, so we decided it would be fun to cross from one tree to another and Ward wanted to go first. There ordinarily would have been no problem, but this time someone had partially cut the limb through and as Ward crossed to the other tree, it broke and Ward fell fifteen feet, breaking both arms above the wrist, dislocating his left elbow, and breaking his right elbow. He spent many painful days in our main bedroom recovering. He was less fortunate than I as he was never able to bend his right arm more than one fourth the way.

But Ward was not the last of my friends to find shelter in our home. While I was a student at Hillsborough High in Tampa during the winter of 1937-38, I had a close friend named Jack Young. The exact order of events is now a bit vague but as I recall, Jack's home situation didn't lend itself to many opportunities, so he traveled north with us one year and worked on the farm where my father was manager. Jack lived with us, and we pitched hay together, shared the same bed room, and cleaned the maggot-ridden manure from the barn together. I can still see Jack coming from the springhouse carrying that old white milk pitcher with the crack in the handle - it's still there (the crack, that is) even though we thought it would give way years ago. Jack also became an active participant in "Gospel Echoes," the youth group of the Frazer Church, so we were all surprised and disappointed when he announced one day he was leaving for Oakland, California. In June 1940 Jack sold his 1931 Model A Ford Victoria, be-

lieving that the proceeds would be sufficient to purchase a bicycle and finance his trek to California. However, after negotiating the hills of central Pennsylvania and coasting downhill five miles into Johnstown, reality set in and he traded his bicycle for his thumb. In Detroit he was picked up by a young couple from Tacoma, Washington who had just purchased a new 1940 85 hp Ford. They also had a borrowed 60 hp Ford in Chicago which they picked up and which Jack drove following them hour after hour following that red tail

HOME ON THE ARTHUR GUY FARM, 1938
This farm is located near Malvern, Pennyslvania. My family lived here for several years beginning in 1937. This is where a curious skunk came in the kitchen door early one morning and left his calling card on the floor of the pantry before leaving. The house and our clothing was saturated with the skunk smell. The principal at Berwyn High School thought it a good idea for me to take the rest of the day off. I did so and walked the ten miles home.

light (Ford had only one in 1940) up ahead. From Tacoma Jack hitchhiked to San Francisco spending most of that summer in the Yosemite National Park. When money ran out he contacted my sister, Naomi, for the repayment of a ten dollar loan. On this high stake he headed for Tampa, Florida via hitchhiking and freight trains. In 1941 he joined the Navy, then got married, raised a family, retired, taught school, retired again and still lives in California. I mention Jack Young because he gave to me many pleasant memories by investing a significant part of his life with me and my family. These experiences with Jack also say something about the unpretentiousness and generosity of my parents at a time when they had not that much to be generous with.

THAT'S A LOT OF HAY!, *1938*
My father kneels in front of a load of hay pitched by Jack Young on the Arthur Guy farm.

These were tough times (1932-1935) and when my father would get a little money he would buy flour for my mother to mix with water for flour pancakes. Sometimes he would "borrow" a few ears of corn from a corn field. Times were tough and I can only imagine the pressure my parents were under - they never really did recover from the 1929 "Crash." For years they struggled with a shortage of finances, never being able to get out of debt, always having month left over after the money, and it was not until I was gone from home and they began receiving Social Security that things began improving for them. My father would buy a house, fix it up, paint it and resell it.

In the early 30's neither of my parents was well. In fact, that was one reason they chose to move to Florida. Somewhere around 1930 my mother had what was known as a nervous breakdown, spending some time in a Philadelphia hospital while my sister and I lived with my Aunt Ona & Uncle Frank Smiley in Berwyn for about six months. My father had problems with stomach ulcers which he cured himself by drinking carrot juice he made by grating carrots and draining the juice through flour sacks like we used for making cottage cheese. In spite of these frailties they lived full lives, my mother living to be eighty-one and my father ninety-nine. He was still climbing ladders painting barns in his upper eighties.

I remember, too, when the tide turned on my Aunt Ona and she became sick with Undulant Fever, a disease contracted from cow's milk before the days of pasteurization. She spent the summer in our hammock on the front porch. It was during this illness that her hair turned gray and she had the unusual joy of watching a pair of Chipping Sparrows build their nest from her gray hair in the climbing rose bush on the edge of the porch.

And then there were the Christmases! My sister and I never saw the Christmas Tree until Christmas morning because my parents would put up the tree, decorate it and put out all the gifts after we were off to bed on Christmas Eve. The tree then remained in place until after New Year's Day. There was one Christmas I will always remember. Aunts, uncles and cousins were there, and everyone was in a festive mood but me, because it seemed there were gifts for everyone but me. My disappointment must have showed because someone sent me into the parlor, which was always kept dark, under pretense of getting wrapping paper or something. It was dark and I couldn't find whatever it was so someone went with me to "help," and there, right in front of me with the headlight on, was my bicycle! This was the most important day of my life. I still remember my many false attempts to mount it and to stay upright, partly because it was a little big for me. I finally learned to do it from the well curb and then push off. That bicycle went to Florida with us where I rode it to school, to the doctor's office and paper route, even my father using it by strapping his large camera and tripod to it when there was no money for gas.

NAOMI'S FIRST CHRISTMAS, 1919
At Lemoyne, Pennsylvania

MY FIRST CHRISTMAS,
1921   At Lemoyne.

NAOMI'S SECOND CHRISTMAS, *1920   At Lemoyne. Note the victrola in the corner.*

CHRISTMAS, *1922   At Lemoyne. l-r: Naomi and Lowell.*

CHRISTMAS, *1923*
At Valley Forge.

CHRISTMAS, *1924*
At Valley Forge. The doll cabinet now belongs to our daughter, Ruth.

My mother's oldest sister was Ruth Boyer, who had ten children. Her youngest sister was Ione "Ona" Smiley who had one child, Ione. We also had cousins in New Jersey, and this pretty much comprised our social life, even though my sister and I did not like the New Jersey Bogia cousins because they came from the city and ran all over the place doing sacrilege to our personal places and things. They were like bulls in a china shop. Church was not a factor in our social life either, even though my father would say on occasion, "I think the children should be in Sunday School," and once in awhile he would take us to the St. Matthew's Church (German Reformed) Sunday School, coming for us afterwards. It was in this parking lot I first remember seeing the 1930 Buicks - I don't know why this was important. I also remember singing a verse of "We Three Kings" in a Christmas program at this church. I once attended a Halloween program at our one-room school dressed up as a Fellowship Farms milking hand, complete with three-legged stool from which I kept falling off. I stole the show.

ST. MATTHEWS CHURCH, *1994*
This was the first church experience for my sister and me. It was a German Reformed church but is now a United Church Of Christ. It is on Route 401, right next to our one-room school house. My father would take us and then come for us after the services.

47

ST. MATTHEWS SCHOOL PORTRAIT, *1930*
This is the entire student body. I am on the third row, second from the left.
My sister is on the second row, third from the right.

**UNCLE CHARLES
and AUNT RUTH BOYER**, *1890's*
Aunt Ruth was my mother's oldest sister.

"WATCH THE BIRDIE", *Fall 1921*
Some of my mother's family taken by my father at our home in Lemoyne, Pennyslvania.
l-r: Paul Miller (my half-brother), Uncle Frank Smiley, Aunt Ona Smiley, Ione Smiley, Grandma
Madden (my mother's mother), my mother holding me, Naomi sitting on the porch step.

COUSINS, *late 1920's*
Dorothy & Constance Tripler.
The cousins we played with the most
were these two girls plus Lawrence and
Walter Madden.

COUSINS, *about 1925*
Verna & Francis Miller. They were our only
Lancaster County cousins with whom we had much
opportunity to play. They were the children of my
father's youngest sister, Emma, who lived on Grandpa
Nissley's old homestead.

"LAWRENCE" MADDEN
about 1915
He kneels by my mother's
spinning wheel.

COUSINS, late 1920's
Lawrence & Walter Madden.
They were the children of
Laurie and Alice Madden and
were reared by Aunt Ona &
Uncle Frank Smiley after their
mother, Alice, died.

LAURIE MADDEN, about 1920
Laurie is holding my sister, Naomi,
in Lemoyne, Pennsylvania.

LAWRENCE MADDEN

Mystery surrounds "Laurie", "Lawrence", "Larry" Madden. It is not certain who his parents were but he was born somewhere around 1900 and grew up in my extended Madden family. He was about twenty years my senior and while I don't ever remember meeting him, I am sure I did. I do remember his wife, Alice, and their two sons, Lawrence and Walter Madden. They were two of our favorite cousins with whom we played most often. After their mother died they were raised by my Aunt Ona and Uncle Frank Smiley. Larry grew up in the Malvern/Paoli/Berwyn area, but after Alice's death gravitated toward Philadelphia where he spent most of his life. My sister and I have gotten bits and pieces of strange conversation about Larry but were never curious enough to ask questions when questions should have been asked. The authentic sources for these questions are now long gone.

51

MY FIRST PONY RIDE, 1929

"GIDDYUP", about 1925
I'm riding my Uncle Frank Smiley's ice wagon horse.

52

As I recall it, our social life outside the family was primarily the Ku Klux Klan. I remember attending KKK parades in West Chester with crosses, white hoods, and cross burnings! These were big events with large crowds gathering in fields around West Chester and Downingtown and I remember after one such meeting spotting a man a few cars from us very pale and in obvious pain. My uncle Frank said, "He just broke his arm trying to start his Model T Ford." The KKK was very popular in those days. "Hello Mac" meant, "Make America Catholic" and Hello Kap" meant, "Keep America Protestant." My Uncle always said, "Hello Kap."

The existence of the KKK contributed to the dark side of American history. Fortunately the KKK no longer enjoys the public approbation it did seventy years ago. Unfortunately, it is still alive and while it may not be in good health, it exists.

THREE KKK "SISTERS", 1926
Photo taken at the KKK rally in Washington, D.C.
My mother would be embarrassed by this photo today.

l-r: My mother, Mary Jessica Madden Nissley,
her niece, Helen Boyer Tripler, and her oldest sister,
Ruth Madden Boyer.

KU KLUX KLAN PARADE, 1926
Washington, D. C. rally. Hopefully this kind of acquiescence to hate and racism will never be repeated.

My sister, Naomi and I were pretty normal kids I think. We had our fights, mainly about whose turn it was to wash or dry the dishes. My main complaint when drying was that she would put wet dishes on top of the ones next ready to dry. We created many of our own playthings, our main toy being stick people literally made from sticks - calling them "Little Things." One of our most exciting games was playing, "Going To Florida." It was one-eighth mile from our house to the mail box on Rt. #100 and we would dress up the dolls, put them in our wagon along with the cat, and play we were going to Florida while we went for the mail. It was great fun. We had certain places to camp overnight, setting up camp and tent and of course we took Lady - our dog - along. Now this was not a figment of overactive imaginations. We really did go to Florida. I was just eighteen months old for my first trip - so I'm told - when we went by boat to Jacksonville and then by wood-burning train to Tampa. In fact my father had been going to Florida for many years as a matter of prudent business. Among our prolific collection of family photos is a post card picture of my father standing beside his Pullman car in Birmingham, Alabama. It was a card from my mother to her sister in Pennsylvania on which she referred to my father as "Mr. Nissley." They were working in Birmingham on their way to Florida for the winter season in Tampa, which always seemed to be the destination and, while I don't remember anything from my boat trip, I do have a sizable collection of memories of Florida.

In our early days in Florida (before 1932) we settled in DeSoto Park, a tourist park with a beach on McKay Bay. The park was mostly made up of small one-room frame cottages, a quite attractive park with palm and oak trees and petunias, the fragrance of which even today creates for me visions of DeSoto Park. There was also an attractive pier, small grocery store and a restaurant which my mother operated one

LIGHT SNOW IN BIRMINGHAM*, 1917*
My father stands by the running board. He and my mother stopped in Birmingham, Alabama on their way to Florida.

DESOTO ELEMENTARY SCHOOL, *1995*
This is the school in Tampa, Florida where I attended 68 years ago, from 1927 to 1928.

OUR HOUSECAR TRAILER, *1933*
This is the trailer we lived in during the Summer of 1933. My father pulled it with our 1929 Model A Ford coupe. This is the trailer in which Ward Holloway and I were riding when we were "hit" by the train in Perry, Florida the summer of 1933.

winter with a partner. I'm told that once, when I was six or seven years old, I had an encounter with the local bully - Midge Williams - on the beach. As the story goes, we both took our stance with fists clenched when I suddenly turned and ran away crying, "If I knew what kind of fighter you are, I'd clean up the beach with you." My sister says she remembers defending me by fighting him in the middle of the street. She pulled his hair and scratched him as they rolled around in the sand. The action attracted quite a crowd until Midge's mother broke through the ring of spectators and rescued him.

I also remember the time uncle Frank took me fishing on the 22nd Street bridge which crosses the entrance of McKay Bay. It was a paved bridge with cement railings except for the center span where the road narrowed, and it was made of wood. On this particular day we were fishing on the left side of the bridge when a Model A Ford stake bodied truck hit the wooden railing on our side of the bridge, knocking out the whole front suspension of the truck, then bounced across the road knocking down a fellow fisherman - right across from us - rolling him along with the bumper finally coming to rest on top of him. It was a very bad scene. I can still see that man's mangled face and hear his gurgled breathing. My uncle said, "I think we better go home."

We also lived here in DeSoto Park briefly in 1932 until we bought the house on 15th Street. During that time my half-brother was with us and we played checkers by the hour, but I don't remember ever winning. I do remember rolling his cigarettes using his cigarette machine, a device in which you would place cigarette paper, fill it with tobacco and then pull a handle to roll it together. I remember feeding ants to the doodle bugs (Ant Lions) in the sand under the house. Among our collection of family photos is a picture of me at Desoto Park standing with my bicycle, wearing my first pair of long pants, which I hated because they scratched.

A FEW FRIENDS, *1933*
These are some of my friends, my bicycle, and first pair of long pants.

SWIMMING HOLE, *1933*
This is the Dunellen swimming hole in the Withlacoochee River. l-r: My mother, Lowell (in the water), Ward Holloway, Naomi. We spent two weeks in Dunellen. My father tried to take pictures to earn enough money to get us north to Pennsylvania. He would take pictures without film, use the deposit money to buy film and retake the pictures. It didn't go very well. Valdosta, Georgia was as far north as we got before running out of money and summer. We returned to Tampa, Florida.

UPSTAIRS FLORIDA APARTMENT, *1918*
My mother is upstairs and my father stands by his Pullman Car with his camera.

4112 N. 15TH. ST, TAMPA, FLORIDA*, 1932*
This became our home when we moved from Pennsylvania to Florida in 1932.
I stand with my bicycle and my sister, Naomi, stands behind me.

4112 N. 15TH. ST. TAMPA, FLORIDA*, 1996*

DEEP DIVER, *1933*
This man owned the camp in Dunellen, Florida where we stayed for two weeks. He built the diving helmet from a hot water tank and the rear window from a Model T Ford to retrieve motor boat parts from the Withlacoochee River. His wife stands beside him.

Getting back to the summer of 1933, the farthest north we got that year was Valdosta, Georgia, the hottest place I can remember. We had our housetrailer parked under a scrawny pine tree and it was hot with no moving air, and always these gnats buzzing in front of our eyes.

Before arriving in Valdosta, we spent two weeks in Dunellen, Florida on the Withlacoochee River - a beautiful spot. It was here at Dunellen that I demonstrated my protective instincts with fisticuffs. "Non-resistance" was not yet a part of my vocabulary. On the contrary, I was always told that God gave us fists for a purpose and the purpose at hand was a vulgar remark about my mother by a native fourteen-year-old Florida cracker. I determined it was my responsibility to avenge her good name, so one day I met him with his older brother walking through the little park on the north side of the river. I figured the best strategy would be a surprise attack, so as we approached I hauled off with a left hook. It must

be noted that I was twelve and much smaller than my fourteen year old adversary. We traded punches while he was backing up, out of the park on to the road (US 41) and across the bridge toward his home. By this time a crowd had gathered which included his mother who yelled, "Billy, split his head with a brick"! It was not long after that Billy turned and ran, and I felt proud of my prowess and basked in the warmth of my mother's pride in me. I claim no theological significance to this event. Neither of us hurt each other very much. It was just something that happened while I was a "sinner" and lived by the rules and values of this "wicked" ungodly world.

It was also here at Dunellen that lightning struck our camp. My sister, Naomi, was filing her finger nails at the table outside our trailer when the lightning struck and she received a severe shock and burns around her wrists from a blue flame which encircled them. The Spanish moss on the electrical wires above caught fire, and Lady, our collie, chained to the trailer, broke her chain and streaked for the river. She was gone for three days, returning just thirty minutes before we broke camp to leave.

PACK-UP TIME, *1928*
We're loading the Model T Ford in Tampa, Fla. for the trip north. Note the horseshoe crab on front fender.

58

TIME TO TAKE IT EASY, *1917*
My father relaxes on Stone Mountain,
Georgia.

STONE MOUNTAIN, GEORGIA, *1917*
Note the cotton field in the foreground
and of course my father's Pullman car.

MY MOTHER'S 1916 PULLMAN
CAR, *1917*
My parents each owned identical 1916
Pullman cars. She later traded hers
for a 1918 Saxon.

ORANGES IN FLORIDA, *1917*
My father with his Pullman in Florida. The Pullman was built in York, Pennsylvania from 1905-1917. It enjoyed a positive reputation, winning two gold medals at the Russian Expedition in 1911. This quality was certainly verified by my father's experience as he drove this car for at least five years all over Eastern Pennsylvania, to Birmingham, Alabama, Tampa, Florida, and back.

MY FATHER WITH HIS 1916 PULLMAN, *1917*
In Scranton, Pennsylvania.

FLORIDA'S BEST, *1928*
My mother took this photo of my sister and me in Tampa.

A GOOD CATCH, *1928*
Uncle Frank Smiley and his daughter, Ione, hold a string of fish from the McKay Bay, Tampa, Florida

LIVE OAK, *about 1928*
My father took this photo on the shore of Thonotasassa Lake just east of Tampa, Florida.

On the ground l-r: M mother, Lawrence Madden, Aunt Ona Smiley, Walter Madden, and my sister, Naomi.

In the tree: Ione Smiley and me.

61

When we moved to 4112 N. 15th Street we were just around the corner from the Ida St. Mennonite Church where Levi Glick, and his wife Ella, from Minot, North Dakota, was pastor. The Glicks were very warm and caring people, taking their responsibilities seriously, so when they learned of this new family they made themselves friendly making many visits to our home and we to theirs, and for the first time in our lives, we began attending church. Mary Byer was my first Mennonite Sunday School teacher. Her brother, John, and I became good friends, and in fact some years later I hitchhiked from Paoli, Pennsylvania to Goshen, Indiana to be best man at his wedding.

This friendship with the Glicks led to the eventual baptism of my father, mother and myself in 1934 (I had been baptized earlier as an infant at the Good Samaritan Episcopal Church in Paoli, Pennsylvania, and I still have the certificate of baptism). This for both my parents, especially my mother, was a cleansing experience. Her life in many ways was not easy. Her marriage to my father was the beginning of a more meaningful and stable future and the arrival of my sister and me signaled new hope and a brighter tomorrow. In looking back I know she was very proud of us both especially years later when my sister became an accomplished artist in the New York/Philadelphia art world and when I became an ordained minister. This baptism experience put to rest many fears and I'm sure resolved any lingering feelings of guilt. My sister was in high school, so timing was not the best for her, being reserved for some six years later in Pennsylvania. These relationships were a significant watermark for my family and me and were the direct result of a friendship developed between the Glicks and my mother. I remember her talking to the rest of us about baptism and joining the church, but my sister objected because of the Mennonite clothes and her friends at the nearby Cumberland Presbyterian Church. My father didn't say much even though he supported the idea. My first reaction was, "You mean you're going to wear those funny clothes?" But when she explained this is what the Bible says, I believed her and that settled it for me, but of course I wasn't the one who had to wear the "funny clothes." That came later. However, this was the beginning of a lifetime commitment for me to Christian ministry within the framework of the Mennonite Church. My only previous contact with Mennonites was our occasional visits to my father's family near Lancaster and I can still remember my difficulty distinguishing Mennonite women from Catholic nuns on the streets of Lancaster.

Our response to the Church's invitation was not the result of a great evangelistic sermon, or being led step by step through the Book of John, not that sermons and John are not important, but our acceptance of the call was the response to genuine friendship. No bells or whistles, no fan fare, no flood waters of emotion, but simply a response to the still small voice of the Holy Spirit speaking through two of His most gentle servants. My sister's coming to faith happened several years later in Pennsylvania where the preacher's wife (my future

LEVI & ELLA GLICK, 1933
Levi & Ella were dairy farmers in Minot, North Dakota.
About 1930 they came to Tampa, Florida to pastor
the Ida St. Mennonite Church.

mother-in-law) asked her, "Wouldn't you like to be one of us?" Naomi's response was positive and in retrospect she says, "I certainly did. I remember that I enjoyed and looked forward to going to church - this was new. It has never changed."

That summer (1934) when we returned to Pennsylvania, we lived with my Aunt Ruth who lived in the Malvern/Frazer area, so we began attending the Frazer Mennonite Church which eventually became our long-term church home. Aunt Ruth lived just down the hill from George Malin who also attended the Frazer Church, so George and I became good friends, some calling us "Mutt & Jeff" because George was tall and I came only to just above his elbow. We built dams in the creek and tunnels in the hay bales. George had a cousin who was the daughter of the local preacher, whom I would see at church and on occasion at George's home. I was impressed. In fact he gave a picture of her to me once which I kept in a special place.

In the summer of 1935 my father got a farm management job in the Frazer area and I would walk every day to a job mowing grass, planting garden and painting at the preacher's house. This was a good summer for me. The preacher's daughter would refresh me with raisin-filled cookies and cold milk, and I began building relationships with other youth of the church. It was also the summer I learned to drive, piloting our Model A Ford around the alfalfa field and practicing aiming it between the entrance posts of the garage - not always with the best accuracy.

In the fall of 1936 my sister and I both enrolled at EMS in Harrisonburg Virginia - she was a high school junior and I a sophomore - living in a private home on the edge of campus. This year was a good experience for us both, but for me was not without pain. To be thrust into a highly social environment was a great contrast to my hiding place behind the kitchen stove on Blackhorse Hill. I always seemed embarrassed about

IDA STREET MENNONITE CHURCH AND PARSONAGE, 1933
This is where my father, mother, and myself were baptized in 1934 as we became Mennonites.

something and self-conscious, especially in group settings and at meal time. To hear my own voice has been a long-standing source of embarrassment. Other people always had such insightful ideas and were so articulate in expressing them that I was intimidated to think my puny thoughts would be helpful or even relevant. This was particularly true if the group was an unfamiliar one. After many years, I finally made three observations: First, sometimes intelligent people make ignorant comments. Second, they were not devastated for having said something dumb, and the rest of the group did not beat up on them. Third, there were times I had really helpful insights not expressed by others which engendered positive response when I drummed up the courage to articulate them. Initiating comments still does not come easy for me, and I prefer rather to sit and listen than risk saying the wrong thing.

This was the year I experienced the most defining single event of my life. William Detweiler was the guest evangelist at EMS for the Fall Revivals and I remember how I felt when so many of my acquaintances stood up in public confessing their sins - probably the regular garden variety sins of youth - many of which may actually have been important. But I remember how strange I felt for not having anything to confess. Maybe it was guilt for not feeling guilt. At any rate one night before going to sleep I prayed, "Lord, whatever you want me to do I am willing to do. Use me however you wish." I believe this to be the most meaningful moment of my life, even though it didn't seem so big at the time, and my performance since has come far short of His will. I have returned to this event time and time again over the years for refreshment and reassurance. I believe that of all the books on theology ever written, and all the sermons ever preached on conversion, this is the heart of the matter. The key is commitment.

Jesus put it this way when he said, "Love God with all your heart and your neighbor as yourself." All the rest is detail. I cannot remember ever being afraid of God or to die - not that I ever thought that much about it. As far as I can remember I always wanted to do what God wanted me to do. This to me is the essence of being God's child, and at the age of fifteen, just stepping into adulthood, my conscious verbalization of this was the crowning act.

While our family was not a religious family in the traditional sense, we did have a deep respect for the Bible and awareness of God. My mother told us Bible stories and taught us to pray: "Now I lay me down to sleep, I pray thee Lord my soul to keep. If I should die before I wake, I pray thee Lord, my soul to take", and, while my father was never one to verbalize his faith very much, that it was deep and meaningful is not to be questioned. Our family was a closely knit one and we certainly cared

"MUTT and JEFF", 1936
Tall George Malin stands by me. He became my best friend when we moved to the Frazer, Pennyslvania area in 1934. He was Miriam's first cousin and gave me a picture of her.

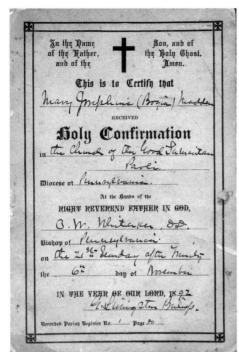

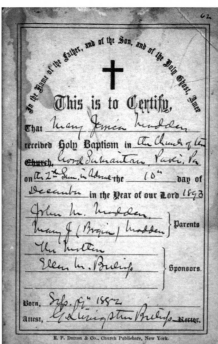

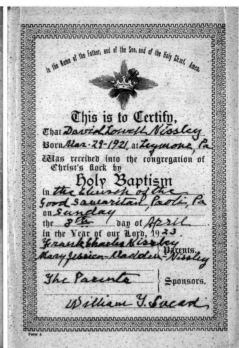

MY GRANDMOTHER'S CERTIFICATE of CONFIR-MATION, 11/6/1892

MY MOTHER'S CERTIFICATE of BAPTISM, 12/10/1893 At age eleven. The Church of The Good Samaritan, Episcopal, Paoli, Pennsylvania. Her mother was confirmed at the same church one year earlier, 12/6/1892.

MY CERTIFICATE of INFANT BAPTISM, 4/8/23

for each other even though there were few outward demonstrations of it. I don't ever remember witnessing any overt expressions of affection between my mother and father or ever hearing them say to us children, "I love you." This may be simply a flaw in my memory. However, I do remember once when I was maybe nine or ten, after some disrespectful words to my father, that my mother reprimanded me by saying, "Your father thinks a lot of you children". But this lack of outward affection was not limited to our family alone. This is the way it was among the families of all our relatives and as far as I could tell, everybody. The "hugging" and "touching" did not become popular in my memory until the late 50's or 60's. I remember how embarrassed I was once in the early 60's at a conference when a female family friend whom we hadn't seen for awhile greeted me with a kiss.

My high school junior year (1937-38) was split between Hillsborough High in Tampa and Berwyn High in Pennsylvania. Because of a job offer to my father in Pennsylvania we planned to leave that year in late February, so I got all my transfer papers from school and checked out, but unfortunately plans changed, and we did not go until a month later, which put me out of school about six weeks before enrolling at Berwyn to finish the last month of the year. This transfer was complicated even more by the lack of equal transfer of courses. For instance, I had not taken American History in Florida so had to catch up the whole semester in the last month.

For my Senior year I went back to EMS and graduated in the same class with the preacher's daughter. My twelve years of education - grade one through high school - took me to ten different schools including three different high schools.

EASTERN MENNONITE COLLEGE, 1940's

EASTERN MENNONITE SCHOOL, *1937*
High School Sophomores.
First Row: Elsie Lehman, Evelyn Brunk, Jacob Batterman, Lowell Nissley, Dwight Hartman, Esther Lehman, Miriam Lehman, Mary Geil.

Middle Row: J. Good, Mildred Good, Virginia Grove, Margaret Horst, Miriam Brackbill, Mary Martin, Harold Ours, Guy Miley.

Back Row: Cleo Weaver, Elwood Weaver, Edwin Keener, Berle Welker, Arthur Kraybill, Maurice Eshleman, Paul Martin.

HILLSBOROUGH HIGH SCHOOL, *1995*
I attended this school in Tampa, Florida for part of my junior year.
My sister, Naomi, graduated here.

CHEERLEADERS, *1938*
Naomi is below the arrow.

67

HILLSBOROUGH HIGH SENIOR, *1938*
Naomi C. Nissley

NINTH GRADE GRADUATION, *1936*
This was my graduation photo from Memorial Junior High in Tampa, Florida. It is the only school I went clear through all grades.

HIGH SCHOOL PROM, *1938*

My sister, Naomi, is dressed in her prom outfit for graduation at the Hillsborough High School.

PAUL DUBOIS MILLER, MY HALF-BROTHER,
late 1930's

MILLER FAMILY PORTRAIT, 1940
Paul Miller my half-brother, with Catherine,
his wife, and their son Paul Miller, Jr.

MY FAMILY, *1942*
Back l-r: Paul DuBois Miller, Sr., Naomi, and my mother, Paul D. Miller Jr., my father and Bobby our collie.

PAUL D. MILLER JR. FAMILY, *1988*
Paul's father, Paul DuBois Miller, was my half-brother. l-r: Karen, Paul D., Berta, Paul Jr., Andrea, Cynthia.

Our trips to Florida had their own mystique and high adventure. Once, when Paul was along, he and I would compete to see who could first identify oncoming cars. I usually won. Today it would be more difficult with the current aerodynamic craze, making them all look like sausages or jelly beans. When driving, Paul would put the "pedal to the metal" for long stretches of time, pushing the `29 Model A Ford full blast, red-lining it to the dizzying speed of 55 m.p.h.! In those days there were no motels and only once in awhile cabins which were one room affairs with a bed costing 50¢ per night. We usually carried a tent, stopping around 4:00 p.m. to camp in a church yard or other wide place along the road. To many, I'm sure, we looked like something from "Grapes of Wrath", with side racks on one running board for luggage and camping gear, our dog and bantam chickens on the other, and spare tires on the back. We felt lucky to make 250 miles per day. There were no Interstates, or, in most places, even paved roads, only dirt/mud or sand trails. We usually followed US #1 or #15 but even then some rivers had to be crossed by ferry.

One of these trips is noteworthy. It was in September of 1934 on our way from Pennsylvania to Florida and involved our 1929 Essex. I don't remember when, where or how we got the Essex but it was a good car with an impressive history. The Essex was born in 1919 to the parents of Hudson whose managers let their fingers walk over the map of England in search of a name with snob appeal. They came up with "Essex." In 1922 it was the first lowest priced closed car in America, selling for $1,495.00. It became very popular and "sold like hotcakes." In 1933 the name was changed to "Hudson Terraplane" until it was dropped from production in 1938.

CAMPING OUT, *1923*
This is one of our family's camping trips. This campsite is at Williamstown, Pennsylvania.

l-r: a neighbor, Naomi, Lowell, my mother, and two neighbors. My father took the picture.

MOTOR HOME, *1923*
This is maybe the world's first motor home, a 1923 Model T. Ford. The photo was taken
beside our house in Lemoyne, Pennyslvania. George Waugaman, a next door neighbor sits
on the hood. Naomi sits on the fender, while I sit on the chair.

Our 1929 Essex was, like I said, a good car but had its own share of problems. By the time we got to northern Florida we had already had fifteen flat tires and a burned-out clutch. We were now going west from Jacksonville intending to intersect with US #41 at Williston which would then be a straight shot south into Tampa. It was 10:00 p.m. with a full moon and my father was driving by moonlight because of a bad generator, putting the lights on only briefly when another car approached. On the edge of Williston he pulled into a filling station for gas. Unfortunately, a police patrol-man was there and asked my father if he was having light problems to which my father explained the bad generator. The patrolman said there was a garage at the corner where #41 went south, and that we should stop and have it fixed. Well, we had already spent our money on tires and a clutch and had no money left for a generator, so when we arrived at the intersection my father headed south for Tampa. We didn't go far until the patrolman stopped us again and in no uncertain terms instructed us to return to the garage. My father made a U-turn but the patrolman went farther down the road to turn around giving us a head start. When we again arrived at the garage intersection, the Essex headed northwest on #41 toward Perry, Florida. Up ahead we could see a sand trail off to the right. We all yelled at my father to turn in, which he did, wheeling into the field not quite on two wheels, stopping maybe 200 yards from the road with lights off. In a few seconds the patrolman went roaring by in his new 1934 Chevy. About 30 minutes later we watched him come slowly back. We sat there swatting mosquitoes until about 3:00 a.m. when we took off again for Tampa.

Speaking of mosquitoes, those were the days before "OFF," even though we did have bottles of Citronella. There was one memorable camping experience when the mosquitoes were so bad that my brother said, "Since all the mosquitoes are inside, I'll sleep outside." So he stuck his head under the tent to the outside where an inquisitive razor back pig soon rooted him in the face. And speaking of pigs, my mother once prevailed upon my father to stop the car because she saw some cute baby pigs along the road. What she did not count on was the protective nature of the mother pig. What happened next was the world's first "Mother's Marathon" around the car - one mother running after the other. The two-legged mother yelled to my father, "On the next time around open the door!"

FAMILY CAMPING, 1923

This campsite was at Honey Brook, Pennsylvania and was shared with my mother's oldest brother, Joseph Madden. Note the Nissley house car in the background.

l-r: Aunt Retta Madden, my mother, my sister (Naomi), myself, and Uncle Joseph Madden.

Portfolio of Photographs
by Frank C. Nissley

NO INTERSTATE! 1917
In the South there were no bridges over many rivers/streams. Here is my
father crossing a southern river via ferry with his 1916 Pullman.

FRANK C. NISSLEY WAS A PHOTOGRAPHER, *1903-1925*

My father used to say he was not bow-legged, that it was the way his tailor made his trousers.
Perhaps the real truth is that his bow-leggedness was due to heavy farm work when a child.
At age twenty-one he traded the tobacco shed for a camera and tripod, and for the next twenty
years traveled throughout the East Coast (mostly the coal regions of Pennsylvania, and Florida)
taking pictures. What he lacked in formal training he made up for with a keen eye for
composition and detail. Never having received adequate recognition for his artistic talent,
I submit the following unidentified photographs from my fathers collection as a tribute to him
for his contribution to our family and to the hundreds of subjects seen through the lens of his
camera. These photos were probably taken in the teens.

GAS & OIL DELIVERY,
1918
Uncle Frank Smiley
stands on his Atlantic Oil Co.
Mack Truck.

LARRY MADDEN,
about 1916

A COAL MINER'S SON

BLIND PEDLER

GENERAL J. B. CARR

VERDENT WOOD

STILL WATERS

*FLOOD
REFLECTIONS*

I LOVE YOU

OUR FUTURE

BOY AND HIS DOG

HOW DO I LOOK?

SHE'S A DOLL

SOMBER FACES

FORTY-TWO STATES

EASTERN STAR
(The women's arm of free masonry.)

HOLSTEIN HERD, *1989*
This painting by my sister, Naomi Nissley Limont, is symbolic of my work as a Dairy Herd Improvement Association (DHIA) tester in Butler County, Pennsylvania during World War II.

LIBERTY BELL, *1946*
This ship was a twin to Cedar Rapids Victory, the ship I sailed on with seven hundred horses for Poland. This photo was taken in the Newport News harbor from the Cedar Rapids Victory. These fast victory ships were built by Kaiser for hauling cargo during World War II.

Memories Beyond Childhood

My FIRST CAR WAS A 1929 DURANT which I bought from my Uncle Frank for $10.00. The Durant (1921-1932) was built by Willy Durant who founded General Motors and lost it twice. Durant was one of American Automobile history's most spectacular and colorful entrepreneurs. The financial crash in 1929 contributed to his bankruptcy in 1936 and death in 1947. Durant production ceased in January of 1932 with some models featuring the industry's first fold down seat backs. I drove mine a few weeks using one gallon of oil for every ten gallons of gasoline, so I sold it to a junk yard in Malvern for $15.00. My second car was a 1933 Chevy 2-door, a graduation gift from my mother. In 1940 I traded it for a 1937 Packard - followed by a variety of twenty-seven additional cars. This car I drove to Florida in January 1942 with my mother and Aunt Ruth to make final settlement on the sale of our house in Tampa. I was not to return to Florida until twenty-six years later in 1968.

In September of 1942 I responded to the invitation of Uncle Sam for CPS (Civilian Public Service) during World War II starting in Luray, Virginia where I was number 32 and where I stayed exactly one year working under Park Forester Bob Moore in the Shenandoah National Park. Because of my tree surgery experience I was put in charge of a small nursery up on the mountain along Skyline Drive, assigned a dump truck and a crew of ten men. In the winter we surveyed stands of White Pine, in the spring pulled gooseberry bushes and in the summer fought forest fires - because of our mobility we were always the first to get called. In bad weather I worked in the drafting room at Park Headquarters making blue prints of forest fire trails. In September 1943 I applied for dairy testing, taking the short course at Pennsylvania State College receiving an assignment in Butler County where I worked until my release in March of 1946, after exactly three years, six months, eighteen days, eleven hours and thirty-three and one-half minutes in CPS. During these days I had sporadic correspondence with the preacher's daughter.

I WAS A TREE SURGEON, 1941

On my twenty-fifth birthday, March 29, 1946, I boarded the Cedar Rapids Victory ship loaded with seven hundred horses bound for Poland. The first half-hour on board a friend and I were going down into the first hold when I made a misstep falling all the way to the bottom hold, badly spraining my right ankle. I was taken to the captain's office where I could hear the sirens of the navy first-aid boat racing through the harbor to my rescue. Talk about feeling important! I was given two choices, either go home or sign a medical release from future liability. I signed the release and was assigned the care of seventy horses on top deck excusing me from going up and down into the hold. It was a rough trip encountering a very bad storm just three days out. The waves were so high you could stand on the rear deck, peer over the rail and watch the propellers turning freely in the air. A few minutes later the deck would be covered with five feet of water. The first day

Continued on page 91

WOMEN'S SECTION, *1940*

Here is part of the women's section of "Gospel Echoes". The photo was taken at George Malin's home. l-r: Lillian Hinkels, Iris Miller, Emily Phenneger, Cora King, Evelyn King, Mary Florence Shenk, Becky Hinkels, Beulah Brunk, Miriam Phenneger, Grace Brunk, Virginia Mosteller, Miriam Brackbill, Catherine Malin, Naomi Nissley, Wanda Baugher, Ruth Brackbill, Dorothy Malin, Mabel Eshelman.

MEN'S SECTION, *1940*

The youth group of the Frazer Mennonite Church was called, "Gospel Echoes", the name suggested by my mother. This is part of the male section. l-r: Emerson Miller, Emery King, Arthur Smoker, George Malin, Lowell Nissley, Wilson Brunk.

CIVILIAN PUBLIC SERVICE CAMP #45, *1943*
This is a view of our camp from up on the hill. We did our own laundry.

DIGNIFIED CAMPERS POSE WITH A SPECIAL GUEST, *1943*
Civilian Public Service (CPS) was the US Government's recognition of conscience by offering civilian service in lieu of the military during World War II. I was the 32nd camper to arrive at Camp #45 Luray, Virginia, on September 2, 1942. l-r: Paul W. McCullough, Ray M. Zercher, C. Arthur Wolgemuth, Abram S. Hoffer, C. N. Hostetter (President of Messiah College), Isaac W. Helfrick, E. David Graybill, John H. Hoffman, Jr., Henry ("Hank") Miller, Paul D. Crider.
C. N. Hostetter was a guest at the camp being a roving pastor for Brethren in Christ CPS men.

FIRE FIGHTING CREW and TRUCK, *1943*
Because our crew was small and versatile we were always the first to be called when there was a fire. During the fire season of 1942-43 we were on every fire but one. Sometimes we worked as long as 36 hours straight.

ABANDONED MOUNTAIN CEMETERY, *1943*

ORCHARD CREW, *1943*

TYPICAL MOUNTAIN TERRAIN, *1943*
*This is some of the rough country we traveled pulling wild gooseberry bushes
to control blister rust on white pine trees.*

BIG MEADOWS NURSERY CREW, *1943*
*The man on the right is Art Smucker who later became
a chemistry professor at Goshen College, Indiana.
CPS'er unidentified on left.*

GETTING READY FOR WINTER, *1942*
*Two CPS'ers mulch spruce seedlings to prevent
heavy frost from lifting them out of the ground.*

D. H. I. A. TECHNICIANS, *1944*

Dairy Herd Improvement Association is an agricultural program to improve quanity (weight) and quality (% butterfat) of milk and ultimately improve breed selection. The above photos are of my co-workers during WWII when we worked in this program in lieu of military service. I sit on the left by Roy Brubaker. We arrived at the Luray CPS Camp on the same day (September 2, 1942) and left together on the same day one year later to attend the Pennsylvania State College D. H. I. A. short course. Roy worked in Washington County and I in Butler County.

Photo on right: John Brenneman, standing on the left, and I worked in Butler County. We shared a former barber shop "apartment" on weekends due to the war time fuel shortage. I am wearing the typical Mennonite plain coat.

GET THE DRIFT? *1941*
My 1937 Packard Model 120 straight eight. I bought
it in 1940 in Ardmore, Pennsylvania for $350.

SOME NEW WILMINGTON FRIENDS, *1944*
In September 1943 I transferred to the Dairy Testing Unit #100 in Butler Co. Pennsylvania.
On weekends we gathered in New Wilmington for worship and socializing. Here I stand with a
few new friends. l-r: Bernice Detweiler, Lloyd Lefever, Lowell Nissley, Herb Zook,
Esther Detweiler and my 1935 Pontiac, "Gray Goose".

on board - after leaving Newport News Harbor - I ate supper five times and I can't say that I ever felt really good throughout the entire trip except when fully relaxed in my hammock swaying with the motion of the ship. We lost one hundred- twenty horses which were thrown overboard. Besides the $150.00 paid me by UNRA, this voyage reimbursed me many times over with vivid images of the English Channel, Kiel Canal, North Sea, and Gdansk (formerly Danzig).

That fall (1946) I enrolled at Eastern Mennonite University (formerly EMC) in the same class with the preacher's daughter, not sure I could even do college work. I shared my misgivings with President John Mumau who gave me some good counsel, advising me to select a subject I liked and give it special attention, so I chose biology and it worked. It seemed easier for me to remember natural science material than theological. In fact there was a time I considered applying for a job with the Federal Lamprey control program in Lake Michigan. Lampreys are a parasitic fish which attack game fish. But in those days the options for a male student in a Mennonite college were limited to either medicine, teaching, or "Christian Service" and since I wasn't very motivated by the sight of blood, and teaching was too intimidating, I chose "Christian Service." The testimony of a Catholic priest I heard recently reflected my dilemma, when he said he was torn between scientific research and theology. So he sought the counsel of an older Bishop who said, "You will have to decide between being a pastor or a Pasteur." Four years later I graduated - along with the preacher's daughter - with a Bachelor's degree in Bible. By now, if anyone is guessing that I've been not so subtly working up to some great announcement, they are right. On July 5, 1947 the preacher's daughter, Miriam Alberta Brackbill, and I were married at the home of the bride by the father of the bride near Malvern, Pennsylvania.

Milton Brackbill, father of the bride, was only the second Man-Of-The-Cloth to influence my life. In fact he became a continuing mentor, confidant, father-in-law and guiding star. I did not always take his advice but I guess we're even. He didn't take mine either. We always respected each other's opinions and points of view and I think mutually profited from each other. While in CPS camp at Luray, Virginia, following some public speaking events, I was told I sounded like Milton Brackbill. Not having many preachers in my life, this was a natural consequence and distinct compliment.

I remember Daddy's words to me once while still in CPS. I was just arriving home for a short furlough and met him in the driveway by the cider press where we talked through the window of the car. He suggested that if there would be a wedding I might be able to get an early release. I have no idea how I replied but there was no question about my feelings for the preacher's daughter, and it was reassuring to know that I had approval rating in high places. What I was not so sure of was my rating among the competition.

I also remember a brief conversation with Daddy, while a student at Eastern Baptist Seminary in Philadelphia. Our men's choir was ready to leave on tour when I showed up one day at the Brackbill home sporting a lapel coat and tie, upon which Daddy informed me that if I wanted to be used in the Mennonite Church I would need to wear the plain coat. Obviously this was not the kind of scintillating advice I was looking for to propel me into churchmanhood. But one of my many great memories of him, besides his sense of humor, was his natural ability to change with grace and dignity. It was my satisfaction one day six years later in Kansas City to show him how to tie the four-in-hand knot in a neck tie.

Miriam Brackbill (Nissley) has been my untiring inspiration, lover, loyal supporter, laugher at my jokes and creator of memories. Her beautiful character and unselfish devotion to family and church has adorned a priceless legacy upon all those who have been honored to know her. I would not be today what I am (whatever that is) without her. Miriam was my first and really only choice for life together. I remember Crescent Lake in Maine where we camped for a week after our wedding, and I remember visiting Maine again twenty-five years later with our children and how it rained during the night, loosening the tent stakes which subsequently collapsed. We all got wet.

In contrast to my family Miriam's tree has Anabaptist (Mennonite) roots on both sides and emerges from a history of Christian piety and church awareness. Her father was a Mennonite minister of considerable renown along with three of her brothers-in-law and her only male Brackbill cousin, Charles Brackbill, who is now a retired but still active minister of the Presbyterian church in New Jersey. Miriam's oldest sister, Emily, married John H. Shenk who was a radio speaker on the "Rock of Ages", and pastor in Virginia and Florida. Grace married B. Charles Hostetter who was a pastor, radio speaker on the "Mennonite Hour", and educator in Nigeria, Africa. Miriam's youngest sister, Peggy, married Michael Shenk who was a pastor in Florida, West Virginia and educator in Virginia. Betty married Kenneth Leasa who with their family stayed by the "stuff" while all the rest gallivanted around the world doing big things. He and Betty stayed home keeping the proverbial "home fires burning" by operating the motel and all the other "zillion" things necessary to provide a strong home base which in retrospect has proven to be invaluable in preserving a sense of family identity

NEAT DATE PLACE, *1941*
The preacher's daughter and I savored a picnic at this estate along the Philadelphia Main Line where I worked as tree surgeon.

hitched to divine purposes. Among other things Kenneth was a medical student, male nurse, teacher and self-employed trucker. What would we all have done without them!

Betty and Kenneth's son, Varden, has become an authority on family history and the fine points of genealogical study. His genius for detail mixed with a titillating sense of humor keeps anyone on the edge of his/her seat who is privileged enough to be present when he embarks upon some voyage into family past - which he is want to do at the drop of a hat. I will leave it to Varden to write the Brackbill book.

THE PREACHER'S DAUGHTER, *1928*
This photo of Miriam Alberta Brackbill was taken by my father little knowing that one day he would be her father-in-law.

VARDEN LEASA, *1996*

And then there is Anita. Anita Perugganon was a thirteen year old girl without a family living as a foster child with a neighbor. She learned to know Peggy at school and would visit her at home after school or whenever she could find an excuse. One day she said right out, "Why can't I live with you?" And so she did. She became an integral part of the Brackbill family along with her inimitable personality and beautiful soprano voice. Anita is retired in LaJunta, Colorado.

Suffice it to say here that the Brackbill family in its entirety has had and still has an immeasurable positive effect on my life beginning in 1935 when my family moved from Florida to the Malvern, Pennsylvania area and I met the preacher's daughter. When Miriam's mother died in 1989 her parents had been married seventy-three years and the family had grown to a total of one hundred sixteen persons. There were five sons-in-law, forty-five grandchildren, fifty-five great grandchildren and three great, great grandchildren. Miriam's mother was ninety-four years old when she died and held the distinction of being the oldest in the family as well as being the first funeral in the family. Almost three fourths of a century and she was the first to lead the way through the cemetery, across the river Jordan to the Promised Land! Miriam's father died in 1993 at the age of ninety-seven.

THE BRACKBILL FAMILY, *1966*
The Brackbill sisters are celebrating their parents 50th wedding anniversary.

Seated: Mother Ruth and Father Milton Blackbill. Standing Miriam, Emily, Anita, Grace, Betty, Peggy. The photo was taken in the Fellowship Room of the Frazer Mennonite Church at Fraser, Pennyslvania.

MARRIAGE RECORD

COMMONWEALTH OF PENNSYLVANIA
DEPARTMENT OF HEALTH
BUREAU OF VITAL STATISTICS

No. 45858

Name of bridegroom, David L. Nissley   Age, 26
Residence, Malvern Pa R D   Occupation, Student
Color, white   Nativity, Pa. (State or country)   Any prior marriage, no
If prior marriage, how and when dissolved,
Name of person consenting when a minor, (Parent or guardian)
Name of bride, Miriam Brackbill   Age, 26
Residence, Malvern Pa. R D.   Occupation, Student
Color, white   Nativity, Pa. (State or country)   Any prior marriage, no
If prior marriage, how and when dissolved,
Name of person consenting when a minor, (Parent or guardian)
Date of issue of license, July 1 19 47   County of issue, Chester

I HEREBY CERTIFY That the above named persons were by me UNITED IN MARRIAGE
on July 5 1947 at Malvern R.D #2
Milton Brackbill
(Minister of the Gospel, Justice of the Peace, or Magistrate)

This Certificate To Be Given To The Persons Married

OUR MARRIAGE CERTIFICATE, *1947*
David L. Nissley and Miriam Brackbill Nissley

OUR OFFICIAL WEDDING PICTURE, *1947*
*Mr. and Mrs. D. Lowell and Miriam Alberta Brackbill Nissley.
This photo was taken October 1947, three months after our
wedding. Our July photos were unacceptable to us.*

HONEYMOON CAMPSITE, *1947*
*The location was on Crescent Lake
in Maine. The camper was loaned to
us by my parents. The tent folded out
from the side of the camper revealing
a well stocked kitchen. Unfortunately,
one of Miriam's sisters, among other
things, exchanged the pancake mix
for plain flour.*

HAPPY CAMPER!, *1947*

For a time it seemed that Miriam and I were destined to be full-time professional students. Following Civilian Public Service (CPS) in the spring of 1946 I enrolled as a college freshman at Eastern Mennonite University (EMC then). Miriam had already taken one year but following our marriage in 1947, slowed down her academic pace to help finance our scholastic pursuits. We were married in July and that fall of 1947 we moved to Goshen College in Indiana for our sophomore year transferring credits back to EMU for graduation in 1950 - the year of the "Jubilee". That fall (1950), I enrolled in Eastern Baptist Seminary in Philadelphia again transferring credits back to EMU graduating in 1951 with a ThB.

"OAKWOOD" GROUND BREAKING, 1950
Our college class was joined by the high school graduating class in gifting the college a cabin called "Oakwood". This is a building in Park Woods for class reunions and other social activities. John Lederach is handling the wheelbarrow and I wield the shovel. J. Otis Yoder our faculty adviser stands in front of me. Some years later the name was changed to, "College Cabin" following the appropriation of "Oakwood" for a new dormitory. Some students today call it the "Bard's Nest".

Those years in college seemed interminable but in retrospect were invaluable. Being class president and active in campus activities like College Hikers prepared me for leadership roles in a wide variety of settings later on. Our class of 1950 had many unique features not the least of which was our class vice-president, Myron Augsburger, who fifteen years later became president of the college. Our class contained forty seven members of which twelve were married couples and has maintained an unbroken record of an annual class letter. The class aspires to raise an endowment fund of $200,000 by its 50th class reunion in the year 2000. Our class project was "Oakwood" a cabin in the woods for small group meetings.

1950 "JUBILEE CLASS", 1995
The following persons attended our 45th class reunion in October, 1995. Eastern Mennonite University, Harrisonburg, Virginia.

Front row, l-r: D. Lowell Nissley, John K. Brenneman, Paul Glanzer, Esther Wenger, Helen King Yates, Erla Culp

Middle row: Norman Kauffman, James Brunk, Paul T. Yoder, Linden Wenger, Elizabeth Good, Mildred Hostetter, Merna Shank

Back row: Myron Augsburger, James Hess, Isabelle Yoder, J. Otis Yoder, Ellen Kauffman, Miriam Nissley

CRYSTAL SPRINGS MENNONITE CHURCH, *1951*
This church at Crystal Springs, Kansas, was my first pastorate. We moved here in September 1951. This congregation was formerly an Amish Mennonite congregation that met near Inman, Kansas. The building was dismantled and moved to Crystal Springs where it was reassembled as a Mennonite church sometime following the merger of the Amish Mennonite and the Mennonites west of the Mississippi in 1927.

Memories of Christian Service

After GRADUATION in 1950 with a B.A. (and Miriam also with her B.A.) and again in 1951 with a Th.B., we went to Crystal Springs, Kansas where we served four years as pastor, and where both our children were born, Dale in 1951 and Ruth in 1954. They have both been a joy and have given us reams of memories over the years. I remember the kindness to Miriam and genuine helpfulness of the church when they both were born.

Crystal Springs was a place of many beginnings for us. It was my first pastorate and the place where I preached my first real sermon. Our first child, Dale, was born here with Ruth arriving three years later. I conducted my first wedding (Betty Ann Burkholder to Lyle Shetler) and first funeral (Grandma Schindler) here and the parsonage was the first house of our marriage. Previously we were either apartment dwellers on a college campus or living at Miriam's home between academics. It was my first experience at welding - I worked part time for Norman Miller, the local blacksmith. It was also our first experience in Kansas - west of the Mississippi River. However, most important of all, Crystal Springs is where we made our first great friends in the Midwest. It is hard to explain but among these people we found a freshness and unpretentious friendliness not found everywhere. Perhaps it's because they live so close to their history of dust bowls, drought and multiple crop failures.

I remember Gladys Troyer. Each year several women from the Crystal Springs Church would conduct a Bible School at Rago, Kansas, a small community about fifteen miles north of Harper, Kansas. In addition to classes for the children, there was an adult class for their mothers. One of these mothers was Gladys Troyer, and for the first time in her life, she saw herself in need of what only God through the Holy Spirit could provide. She became a Christian. She had a husband (Vern) and five children (twin girls and three boys) and wanted to be baptized to become a part of the Christian community at Crystal Springs.

THE PREACHER'S DAUGHTER, *1934*
This was the year Miriam & I first met.

Even Vern who had Mennonite roots wanted to renew his fellowship with the church. Everyone rejoiced at the return of the "Prodigal Son" who in this case also brought along a wife. In reality the wife brought him, but anyway, here was a whole family coming into the fellowship of the church, and for a small country church in the wheat fields of Kansas, this was no small event, for which everyone rejoiced until one day during instruction. The day which was so bright and full of promise turned into a storm of controversy. Vern had been previously married and divorced. It happened when he was eighteen and the marriage lasted only a short time with no children involved, and Gladys didn't even know of it until years later when she found some papers in a dresser drawer. No one questioned the sincerity of Glady's and Vern's new found faith, but there surfaced the familiar questions like, "Let them

98

join the Baptist Church," to which Gladys replied, "I don't know anyone at the Baptist Church and besides I became a Christian through the witness of the Crystal Springs Mennonite Church and if I can be a Christian in the Baptist Church why can't I be one in the Mennonite Church?" Divorce is a multifaceted issue, answers for which I certainly did not have. But one question plagued me then and still does: Since everyone agreed that Gladys and Vern were Christians and that God, therefore, had received them into His fellowship, who were we to exclude them from ours? The following year "Divorce" was on the agenda of the South Central Mennonite Conference which resulted in the decentralization of decisions on divorce, giving every Overseer freedom to deal with each case on its own merits. Gladys and Vern were received into church fellowship but with uneasy feelings on the part of many. In fact it must be honestly said that Gladys and Vern were never made to feel really welcome, and a few years later moved to Hutchinson, Kansas and joined the Mennonite Church there.

For the most part Mennonites have made peace, albeit an uneasy one, with the divorce issue. Unfortunately, the legalistic view of the Church which became so problematic with divorce is still alive and well, with only the labels being changed to "Homosexual" and "Members of the Military." Should the goal be church purity or should the church be an instrument of God's grace in the lives of all men and women seeking more perfectly the will of God?

Now Gladys Troyer was an "outsider" but so was Jay Whitwill, except that Jay created a whole different set of memories for me as well as the Crystal Springs Church. That cold, cloudy November day in 1952 with snow in the air, and Jay marching coatless, his navy cap inside out, before a drawn pistol to the brig will always be in my memory.

Jay was a young Baptist from Texas, who, because of the precedent of his father and older brother, joined the navy in 1951. While stationed in Bainbridge, Maryland, he by providence learned to know the Mennonites of Lancaster County, Pennsylvania and this chance encounter changed his life forever. He would hitchhike to Lancaster on weekends, staying with the Jonas Heisey family and attending church with them at the Kauffman Church. He became a close friend with Jay Oberholtzer, a young man about the same age, who gave him - at Jay's request - books on peace, the peace movement, Mennonite history, and the conscientious objector movement. When Jay was transferred to Corpus Christi, Texas, he made contact with Mennonites around Premont and Alice, from here making a trip to Mennonite Central Committee in Pennsylvania where he officially filed for CO status. Navy officials in Texas, however, apparently not knowing how to handle this strange request, shipped him to the

CRYSTAL SPRINGS, KANSAS, 1971
This photo was taken from the top of the local grain elevator.

99

JAY WHITWILL, 1950's

Ever since the Fall of 1951 when I first met Jay at the Hutchinson, Kansas Naval Airbase, he has been my great friend. He is a Texan, a Southern Baptist, a budding Naval Pharmacist, a conscientious objector, a nurse, a world traveller, a realist optimist --- friendly but not patronizing, generous but not gratuitous, simple but not simplistic, Christian but not pious.

Naval Air Base at Hutchinson, Kansas where I learned to know him. He would spend weekends with us and in the process worked his way into the hearts of the whole Crystal Springs congregation.

That cold day in November 1952 began a very difficult journey for Jay. Jay said he was drugged and put in a straight jacket because he refused any longer to take orders. Since he had exhausted all appeals for conscientious objector status he finally decided that this was the only way. At 8:00 one morning, I received a phone call from Jay, "I have been arrested and am due for Captain's Mast at 10:00. Can you come up and get some of my things?"

The hearing took place in a bare room with only a lectern in the center. I stood along one wall with Jay and two other sailors, who had been arrested for hunting jack rabbits on the runway. Along the left wall stood five or six naval officers. A Navy Yeoman gave

some procedural instructions and was immediately followed by the entrance of the Commanding Officer. The "Defendants" were ordered to remove their caps and turn them inside out - a sign of disgrace. The rabbit hunters were ordered to step forward seven paces, were charged and summarily sentenced. Jay's turn was next. After his seven paces, the CO made no attempt to hide his anger with Jay's actions. However, the naval officers, when given opportunity to "testify," spoke very highly of Jay's work (pharmacy), and of him as a person. When Jay was asked if he had anything to say, he requested that his civilian witness be heard and I was given opportunity to express appreciation for Jay and the sincerity of his convictions. The CO then took a letter from his pocket written to the navy by Jay's mother in which she blamed the Mennonites for "brain washing" her son. Jay said later this was a complete shock to him, for he had no idea that his mother had written to the Navy. He was sent twice to the Naval mental hospital in Memphis, Tennessee where Jay said he was kept in locked security. One and a half years later he was given an honorable discharge, after which he enrolled in the nursing program at Belleview Hospital in New York, earning his nursing degree. He then began private duty nursing in New York with one stretch in Central America with Exxon Oil Company. He took these opportunities to make friends world wide, whom he would later visit. Jay was a good nurse and made good money, which he spent not on "things," but to finance trips to Japan, Africa and India for months at a time doing voluntary service at mission stations, and visiting his international friends. Jay is now retired in Tulsa, Oklahoma.

ARGENTINE MENNONITE CHURCH, *1955*
This was my second pastorate, located at 3701 Metropolitan Ave., Kansas City, Kansas.

I remember riding in the car with Milo Kauffman on US Highway #160 between Winfield, Kansas and Crystal Springs. By now I had been pastor at Crystal four years and was considering asking for a leave of absence to finish my Master's at Eastern Baptist Seminary in Philadelphia, but Milo suggested that I consider instead the Argentine Mennonite Church in Kansas City and that I finish my Seminary work at Central Baptist Seminary there (which I later did in 1962). Frank Raber was pastor at Argentine, but had developed a heart condition and was advised by his doctor to retire. I shared with Milo my convictions, or lack thereof, for the "plain coat" - which I still wore - and wasn't exactly thrilled about moving into a large metropolitan area and to be a walking advertisement for the Catholic Church. He assured me that many things had changed at the Argentine Church and that the plain coat should not be a problem. As it turned out, the Argentine Mennonite Church had not changed all that much, but was in fact a rural church in the city with many long-standing internal problems, not the least of which was the continued residence of a former pastor with his family and followers. Miriam and I arrived in August, 1955, with Dale (four), and Ruth (one) and Bobby, our collie. We arrived bright-eyed, youthful, a bit anxious, energetic and idealistic with scads of ideas of what the church should be in the city. Ironically, just four years earlier on our way to Crystal Springs, we stopped in Kansas City to visit Maynard and Margaret Yoder, former classmates at EMU (EMC then). It was just after the Kansas City flood and our hosts treated us to a tour of the town. After leaving Kansas City heading southwest to the wheat country of Southern Kansas, we thanked God for not calling us to the city. Now here we were smack dab in the middle of where we had thanked God for not leading us. God truly moves in mysterious ways.

We should have known better, but diplomacy has never been one of my strong points. We were told, and believed, that the key to a successful church was the pastor, that basically people wanted to know the truth and would accept it if only the pastor had the insight and courage to talk about it. Courage we had, but insight was more like tunnel vision. Our first clue was when we proposed a visitation program to new residents moving into the community. I had read somewhere that people would establish their church, shopping and so-cial habits within the first six months of a major move and this seemed to me a good rationale for involving the church in what it was supposed to be about, thus making ourselves friendly, and maybe, just maybe, some at least would come and give us a try. This prospect threatened some in the church and the effort fizzled after just a few weeks. In time we figured out that many believed what we said was true, and that some of these newcomers would actually come to church - along with their divorces and embarrassing questions which the church either could not or would not answer. One Sunday morning, I took my non-diplomatic skills to a new height by appearing in the pulpit clad in a lapel coat and tie and a sermon titled, "The Christian Attitude Toward Change." That afternoon one sister explained to me on the phone for *one and a half hours* how that there were no ministers in all of the Iowa/Nebraska Conference who did not wear the plain coat. She came from Nebraska.

Another signal event was the "Mother's Room." The Church Council proposed closing in the rear cloak room to make a convenient place for mothers to take their small children. This was one of those things where the need was so obvious and the cost so minimal, one would expect, "Why didn't we think of that before?" I was totally shocked by the opposition. One sister said, "I changed my babies on the bench in the basement, and the mothers today can do the same." When it came to a church vote the mothers' room won, but was another stitch in the "Mennonite Curtain" dividing the congregation, the Church Council winning the battle, but ultimately losing the war. This event of itself was not all that important except that it illustrates the need for patience and dialogue in the business of nurturing God's people and building His Church. A few more months living with the idea might very well have yielded a consensus of opinion or at least sufficient agreement for everyone to feel good about.

Not all memories of the Argentine, however, should be forgotten. Most of them were of people who became our lifelong close friends, who were supportive and committed to being God's people in a world where in His providence He had placed them, and there were many other good memories as well: the neighbors next door, our first new car, and the exposure to a large metropolitan community with the Arts, Drama, and the vibes of an exciting, growing community. After two years at the

GRACE MENNONITE CHURCH, *1960*
This is the site of my third pastorate. It was located at 5700 Nall Ave. Mission,
Kansas, a suburb of Kansas City.

Argentine Church, the Grace Mennonite Church formed and we moved five miles south to Mission, Kansas - a Kansas City suburb. I found it hard to believe that a church split could occur in our time, because these were things we read about in church history and were not the stuff from which the Church is made in the 1950's. I was sick in bed with the flu the night the vote was taken on my tenure, but two sisters of the Church came by after the meeting to report that I lost the vote 49 to 51. One of them said she voted "No" because she knew I couldn't stay anyway and she was right. I remember how I felt several years later in a pastoral counseling class at the Seminary where we were discussing why people do what they do. It was as though a pair of huge double doors had been flung open upon a vast new world! Oh, if only I had had that insight before!

The pastor of the Methodist Church down the street, whom I learned to know in the local Ministerium, offered me the Associate Pastorate of their church, because he said, "We are looking for someone; and, in a couple of years you could have a congregation of your own." About a year later that pastor died suddenly of a heart attack, and God only knows what the succeeding decades would have been if I had accepted, but God in His providence has never seen fit to tell me. We decided that the problems in the Argentine were not endemic to the whole Mennonite Church and that we would still cast our lot with those we knew and whose values we shared. So, when several families came to us and said they were not prepared to stay with the Argentine Church regardless of what we do, they asked us to consider helping them plant a new congregation in another part of town, and we agreed.

I remember the Easter morning breakfasts the Grace Mennonite enjoyed each year after the sunrise services. I remember the meetings of our Church Council around our dining room table and the inadequacy of our window air conditioner, and Joan Williams from across the street with her daily coffee pot in our kitchen.

────────────

I remember the day when Robert Brown* came to the parsonage with Mary* to get married - that day. I congratulated them but suggested they schedule several counseling sessions first. Robert finally agreed but Mary refused because she was on parole and pregnant. They went elsewhere and were married that same day. I remember the three AM phone call three years later from Robert's extremely distraught sister, Sue*, who asked me to come to their home. Robert had just shot Mary. It had been a stormy marriage and they had been separated for some time. Mary was pregnant and she would taunt Robert by saying it wasn't his baby. Mary and her two children were living with Sarah*, her mother-in-law. Robert came home that morning and shot Mary with a .22 pistol while she slept in the same bed with Sarah and one of her children. The funeral for Mary was one of the most difficult for me even though my funeral sermons seemed to elicit the most affirmation and expressions of helpfulness. Robert was present under heavy guard. There was a trial and Robert was sentenced to life imprisonment.

I remember the conversations Stan Bohn and I had

traveling to and from the tornado cleanup at Meriden, Kansas in 1963. Stan was pastor of the General Conference Mennonite Church in Kansas City and I was pastor of the South Central Conference, Grace Mennonite Church. These discussions led to the eventual merger of the two congregations into the Rainbow Boulevard Mennonite Church, maintaining dual membership in both GC and MC Conferences, and to my knowledge, the first to pioneer this relationship, there now being eighty-nine such congregations (1994). Following this merger, I accepted a position with Mennonite Mutual Aid in Goshen, Indiana as Director of Field Services, and I must admit this was a traumatic decision - to leave beautiful Kansas City for a Mennonite "ghetto" in Indiana was not a jump-up-and-down-with-joy kind of prospect for us. Actually, one day I slumped down in the empty closet of what had been the study, and cried. I was there in this empty house all by myself loading up the trailer for the final load, when the memories of this house, the Church, the rose bushes, the neighbors, be-

GRACE MENNONITE CHURCH INTERIOR, 1960

CHARTER MEMBERS OF GRACE YOUTH FELLOWSHIP, *1958*
l-r: Connie Sandvold, Roy King, Carol King, Marjorie King.

FIRST PASTOR'S COUNCIL, *1958*
The Church Council usually met in our home.

l-r: Melvin Buller, Roy King, Lowell Nissley, Ora Troyer, Dan King.

came overwhelming. Our move was scattered over the spring and early summer months of 1964 and we soon discovered that it is not the place that makes a place but the people of the place.

The ten years we lived in Goshen were replete with good memories. Eight of these years were spent with Mennonite Mutual Aid as Director of Field Services. It was during this time that MMA became MMAA - Mennonite Mutual Aid Association, an official Fraternal legal entity. This change in organization allowed MMA, among other things, to make legal financial grants to churches and church agencies in lieu of taxes. While here at MMAA I had the satisfaction of creating CHIP (Congregational Health Improvement Program) which gave financial aid to members of low income congrega-

OUR FAMILY, *1956*
We are posing in front of the church parsonage.

l-r: Dale, Ruth, Miriam and "Rev. Nissley" and "Bobby".

tions. I was also the charter editor of the Sharing Magazine. My position at MMAA afforded the privilege of visiting many congregations and conferences across the country from East to West, and from North to South making the case for the sharing of resources with one another. Leaving MMAA was a painful, experience because I enjoyed the challenge and felt that MMAA had a great future in serving the interests of stewardship and corporate compassion throughout the entire Anabaptist church family. It was and is unfortunate that the dark side of human nature is always with us. Wouldn't it be great if the church could at least find ways to resolve conflicts within the parameters of professional churchmanship and Christian grace?

It was in Goshen that we tried our hands as restauranteurs. I spent three months remodeling the old historic Waterford Mills Store which also became the life span of our restaurant. We opened in October, 1973 and sold it December of the same year. Unfortunately, we had insufficient capital and experience to allow for any mistakes. These three months yielded not only some deep dark emotional valleys but some joyous mountain tops as well. Our employees from cooks to dish washers to waitresses/waiters were very supportive, loyal and willingly sacrificed personal time and income to help in our final days. The restaurant has had several owners since, plus a fire.

It was in Goshen I racked up many miles of memories (nearly 10,000 per month) pulling a forty-foot lowboy behind an International tractor for Coachmen Industries, delivering recreational vehicles. I stopped at every truck stop between Indiana and California, Texas and Halifax, and every other restaurant, and in the process stopping at or going through every state but five, plus four Canadian Provinces. I remember being snowbound in Cheyenne for three days and the 25 below zero delivery in Fargo, North Dakota. My memory banks will always retain the last trip to Halifax and the Lowell, Massachusetts bypass. A passing motorist sounded his horn and a glance in the mirror showed smoke coming from the right rear wheel of the trailer. The wheel bearing had burned out, allowing the wheel to come off and bounce back and forth between the guardrail and the trailer. As I passed by, the wheel crossed all three lanes of traffic, coming to rest in the median so hot it set the grass on fire. I retrieved the wheel and limped off at the

I WAS A TRUCK DRIVER, 3/27/73
My final truck driving stint was with Coachmen
Industries out of Middlebury, Indiana. In this photo
I'm filling out my log book at Olney, Texas. The truck
is an International series 1700.

next exit to a wide place along the road to make temporary repairs. I replaced the hub, but the axle threads were so badly stripped the best I could do was a cotter key to hold the wheel on for the next hundred miles to a machine shop to rethread the axle. One of the most memorable strokings of my ego also came while working for Coachmen. It was at the Coachmen drivers' Christmas party in 1973 where all forty of us were given a banquet dinner and awards. It was a huge surprise and honor to receive the coveted "Driver of the Year" award.

It was in Goshen that Miriam added a B.S. degree in Elementary Education to her already earned B.A. (Bible), and then taught third grade in the Goshen School system for seven years. In addition to teaching full time and managing our household, she earned her Masters in Education from the University of Indiana.

Some of my best professional memories came from my eight years as Development Officer for Berea College in Berea, Kentucky. I represented the College in nine Southeastern States and is why we moved back, in a sense, to my roots in Florida in 1974, because most of the people I would visit lived in Florida. Berea College is one of those rare and special places in the world of education where the ideals and objectives were easy to talk about. People would often say to me, after their first visit to campus, "The half has not been told." It felt good to have a small part in creating memories for hundreds of talented young people who otherwise would have no educational opportunity.

Upon arriving home one weekend I learned of a phone call from the new President of Hesston College. It was an invitation to come to Hesston and give direction to the reorganization of the Development Department. After several trips to campus and counseling with knowledgeable friends we traded beloved Berea in Kentucky for Hesston College in Kansas from which Miriam and I had both previously accumulated some beautiful memories and where both our children graduated. Hesston's unique blend of Head (Liberal Arts), Hands (Vocational), and Heart (Bible) presents a powerful appeal to a broad cross section of the job market, educating not only the hands but head and heart as well, with it's non-apologetic balance between Bible/ Liberal Arts/Vocational curriculum.

In 1983 we had an opportunity to move back home to Sarasota to direct a new Voluntary Service program for the Mennonite Board of Missions and Charities. It was called VWAP (Vacation With a Purpose) targeting persons (not only retired) who desired a few weeks or months in Florida without getting bored lolling on the beach, playing shuffleboard, golf or eating out with friends. We provided opportunities throughout the State for voluntary service in nursing homes, Habitat construction, social work, medical records or other services with which the volunteers had experience or skills.

It was during this time that Miriam worked at Sunnyside Nursing Home and I was Director of Development for Sarasota County Hospice, to help defray operating expenses for the Mission Board.

A number of miscellaneous jobs followed VWAP. For one season I drove the nurse truck for Sarasota County Mosquito Control supplying spray material for the helicopter as we sprayed during the night for night-time mosquitos. We used 1.6 ounces per acre and some nights would use up to 43 gallons of spray.

Following the control of mosquitos I worked for Sisters & Brothers raising funds for the production of "The Radicals", a historic film portraying the 16th Century struggles of faith of the Anabaptists in Eastern Europe.

CYPRESS GARDENS, 1948
In June of 1948 Miriam & I, Sam & Elizabeth Horst, and six other persons took a trip to Florida
in search of housing for our Junior year at Goshen College in Goshen, Indiana. On the left:
Nissley's '38 Chevy and Ventura Trailer. On the right: the Horst's '37 Chevy and Spartan Trailer.

BOK TOWER, FLORIDA, *1948*
l-r: Elsie Petersheim, Ivan Magal, Gordon Shantz, Ada Zimmerman, Esther Becker, Sam Horst,
Miriam Nissley, Elizabeth Good, Lowell Nissley, Naomi Kennel.

AN ACADEMIC SETTING, *1949*
Our beloved 1938 Chevy and the Ventura trailer. Our home away from home in Park Woods
at Eastern Mennonite University, Harrisonburg, Virginia.

Memories of the Southeast Mennonite Conference

WHEN WE MOVED TO FLORIDA IN 1974, we knew little about the Mennonite churches in Florida except that there were the Ashton, Tuttle, and Bayshore congregations. Since I was traveling a lot for Berea College and mostly home only on weekends, our involvement with a local church was minimal. We did gradually become active through the Tuttle Avenue Church and after several years I was elected Moderator of the Southeast Mennonite Conference in 1986 for a three year term. This was a great experience for me because this kind of thing was a first exposure to the Mennonite Church at large - from an inside perspective - by attending church-wide meetings and becoming a member of the Mennonite General Board, and I didn't even wear a plain coat. This Conference Moderator bit was also a growing experience helping me discover some things about myself I sort of knew before but now were verified, namely, that I do in fact from time to time hatch out some creative ideas, but implementing them is often less creative. I need to learn that it takes patience and time for seeds to germinate, grow and eventually bear fruit. I have believed - and still do - that the Southeast Mennonite Conference has great long-term potential, but in my opinion lacks a matching vision. Sarasota in particular has the seeds for a significant Mennonite center not an enclave or ghetto, but a presence affecting the entire community with the values to which Mennonites are committed. Can it be that Mennonites are afraid of the brightness of their own light? The latent gifts, talents and resources are dormant waiting for the latter rains of vision to make them grow, bloom and bear fruit. No group will ever, in my opinion, rise higher than its expectations, but unfortunately, too often churches move from crisis to crisis rather than lifting up their eyes to view the horizon.

As Moderator of Conference and Editor of the Conference Messenger, I am indebted to the pastors of the Conference, the Executive Committee and a host of others for their patience and continued respect and love.

JAN GLEYSTEEN, 1988
Jan is a Mennonite artist, photographer, story teller and friend. He was born in Holland growing up in Amsterdam during the World War II German occupation during which time his parents successfully hid fleeing Jews in their home. Jan has travelled Europe by foot, bike, bus, car and train and is knowledgeable about most any European subject especially Anabaptist history. He was a fine, knowledgable tour guide for our daughter, Ruth, in her earlier tours and for us in 1988.

OUR DAUGHTER RUTH (after graduation from Berea College with a degree in sociology) was inspired by two Tourmagination trips to Europe, with Jan Gleysteen, to explore the mysteries of theology and the paradoxes of Churchmanship, oops!, I mean Churchwomanship, at Associated Mennonite Biblical Seminaries in Elkhart, Indiana. The encouragement of Jan Glysteen along with the Tourmagination trips, by bus and bicycle, ignited a latent spark of interest in Anabaptist history - thus her trek to AMBS. Those trips also led her to twist her brother's arm to help finance a 40th Anniversary gift to Miriam and me for a Tourmagination trip to Europe in 1988.

It wasn't long however before the survival instincts of a single, free-spirited, independent, young woman found resonance in Respiratory Therapy where Ruth has worked for the past thirteen years at the Venice Hospital plus several nursing homes in Sarasota. She now owns her own home. It has been and is great to have her close by. We love her very much.

Dale, our son, on the other hand traveled a quite different road. After graduation from Goshen College, Indiana, he hitchhiked through Europe and then lit out for Canton, Ohio to seek his fortune with the Canton YMCA as a Voluntary Service worker in youth work. After marrying the YMCA Girls Director, Garnet Pfyle, he discovered that administration at a not-for-profit institution was a lot of hard work, demanding, long on hours but short on pay. But he loved it and is now Administrator of the Louisville, Ohio YMCA. Garnet teaches preschoolers in Canton. Tanya, their daughter, is sixteen with visions of a driver's license dancing in her head. Shawn, their son, is twelve, and on the threshold of that great and wondrous, scary but beautiful world called "Teenager". He is "all boy", whatever that means, holding captive in his breast some great teacher, philanthropist, scientist, pastor or someone still unknown trying to get out. In any case I am confident that both Shawn and Tanya will be (they are already) great persons on whatever road their choices take them, and a pleasure to God who made them and has promised to always be with them.

RUTH ANITA NISSLEY, *1992*

DALE RICHARD NISSLEY, *1998*

Life is less complex now even though the best is yet to come, but new memories keep pouring in upon us. It feels good. Aside from the "normal" creaks and rattles associated with higher mileage, Miriam and I are in pretty good shape. We have no secondhand parts. Everything is original equipment - heart, lungs, kidneys, gall bladder, etc. We were delivered fully equipped and everything still works. Our dinners do not move over to make room for pills. In fact we don't use enough drugs in a year to fill line 4 of Schedule A on our IRS Form 1040. I trust we can continue to upgrade our modem to enshrine our memories forever. Our lives together, Miriam's and mine, have been very rewarding with enough humor to brighten up even the darkest valleys. What would we do without laughter? Someone has said, "If we could sit on a fence and watch ourselves go by, we would die laughing".

OUR GRANDCHILDREN, *1991*
Lido Beach, Sarasota, Florida.   Brother and Sister, Shawn and Tanya enjoy the cool surf of one of Florida's finest beaches.

DALE NISSLEY FAMILY, *1996   l-r: Dale, Shawn, Garnett, Tanya.*

111

THE AUTHOR, MIRIAM and RUTH, *1997*
D. Lowell and Miriam Alberta Brackbill Nissley with their daughter, Ruth Anita Nissley.

MUCH DEPENDS ON OUR WORLD VIEW. There has been an endemic view among some people I know that the world is a big bad place from which to be separate. This, in my opinion, is a first cousin to first century Docetism which believed that the world and everything in it is evil. There is another view which believes the world is going from bad to worse and will progressively deteriorate until God is fed up and destroys it all with fire. I suppose if I were a child victimized by war, malnourished, starving in Somalia (or many other places on the globe), and witnessed the brutal murder of both my parents and with no hope for anything better in the future, I may feel the same way. However, as unjust and evil as

our world is, I'm glad I was not born in the Middle Ages.

In my saner moments I remember that the cold war ended without bombs on Moscow or Washington, DC. Apartied died without a blood bath, and who would ever have guessed a few years ago that the tobacco industry would be hanging on the ropes fighting for its survival? In the long haul there is something about the human spirit that eventually rises above its circumstances. And let us not forget that God's Holy Spirit has been and still is administering His Grace among us, and that gives us hope for the future.

FRANK C. NISSLEY, MY FATHER, 1957

MARY JESSICA MADDEN NISSLEY, MY MOTHER, 1958

Photography by Alexander Limont

NISSLEY (NUSSLI) COAT OF ARMS, 1628

Among the treasured ancient and medieval disks exhibited at the Louvre Museum in Paris, France, is the Nussli Amorial disc. This disc is made of artistic stained glass and displays the Nussli (Nissley) Coat-of-Arms, which is dated 1628. It bears the Coat-of-Arms of Martin Nussli, a butcher at Kaltbrunn, located in Canton of Zurich, Switzerland. An account taken from Swiss records states that the disc was presented to Martin Nussli as an award for his championship marksmanship at a shooting contest.

39 years old when I was born
Frank C. Nissley
1882-1981

37 when Frank was born
Jonas L. Nissley
1845-1920

27 when Jonas was born
Samuel E. Nissley
1818-1887
He built the Nissley house and barn in 1860 and 1857 respectively

26 when Samuel was born
Rev. Samuel Nissley
1792-1868

D. Lowell Nissley
1921-___

John Madden
?-Circa 1864

54 when Jessica was born
John Morrow Madden
1828-1906

Mary Jessica Madden
1882-1963
39 when I was born

15 when John was born
Mary Ann Morrow
1813-1878

27 when Jessica was born
Mary Josephine Bogia
1855-1924

41 when Mary was born
Mary McClosky
1772-1860

19 when Mary was born
Ruth DuBois
1836-___

30 when Ruth was born
Amos DuBois
1806-1880

31 when Amos was born
Jacob DuBois
1775-___

DuBois

DUBOIS (DUBWA') COAT OF ARMS, *early 1600's*

Chretien DuBois was a Huguenot gentleman of the family of DuBois having an estate at Wicres in La Bassee, near Lille, in French Flanders. The Coat of Arms probably dates to the early 1600's. The motto "Tiens ta foy" means, "hold to thy faith".

Here are two coats of arms: Nissley (Nussli) Swiss, and DuBois (DuBwa) French. It is important to note that there were many coats of arms even within a given family and any specific coat of arms would not necessarily be THE Coat of Arms for the whole family. The Martin Nussli Coat of Arms, for instance, was designed by Martin Nussli in 1628 but there may have been additional ones by other Nusslin. In any case, I can personally claim the Martin Nussli Coat of Arms and the Chretien DuBois Coat of Arms because I am their descendant.

31 when Samuel was born	54 when Samuel was born	68 when John was born	23 when Ulrich was born	22 when Jacob was born
Bishop Samuel Nissley	**John Nissley**	**Ulrich Nussli**	**Jacob Nussli**	**Martin Nussli**
1761-1838	1707-1789	1639-1717	1616-1645	1594-___
Erisman District Lancaster, PA	Immigrant from Switzerland with brother Jacob	Died at sea on voyage to America	Persecuted for being an Anabaptist. Died in prison. Noted in Martyr's Mirror pp.1120-22	Created family coat of Arms in 1628, now in the Louvre, France

Note: Information from Amos R. Nissley research (1900-23) and Harry Hoyt Nissley research (1948-53).

It is a comforting massage of the ego to trace one's heritage back to some significant personality or famous family. It is also not without risk as one never knows what may fall out of the closet. The tracking of my father (Nissley) and my mother (DuBois) is the work of others and since genealogy is not the primary focus of this book, I lean heavily upon the accuracy of their research knowing that future research may or may not affirm my roots in every detail.

43 when Jacob was born	37 when Cornelius was born	34 when Louis was born	35 when Jacob was born	29 when Louis was born
Cornelius DuBois	**Louis DuBois**	**Jacob DuBois**	**Louis DuBois**	**Chretien DuBois**
1732-1795	1695-1784	1661-1745	1626-1693	1597-before 10/10/1655

Note: Information from William Heidgerd for the DuBois Family Association, 1968.

The DuBois family is one of the oldest of the Noble houses of Conentin in the Duchy of Normandy. There is evidence to suggest that the DuBois family in Normandy may have its roots in French Royalty but owing to the systematic mutilation of the records of Heguenot families of the Nobility neither Chretien's parentage or issue can be definitely proved. A plaque on pew no. 46 in the Pittsgrove Presbyterian Church, Pittsgrove, New Jersey, states, "In Memory of Louis DuBois, a descendent of Emperor Charlemagne". This is a thoughtful gesture but of course cannot be proved. Chretien DuBois joined the Huguenots in the early 1600's and because of religious persecution his sons Louis and Jacques later emigrated to Ulster County, New York in 1660 aboard the ship, "Guilded Otter"..

THE THOMAS ANTIQUE and CLASSIC CAR MUSEUM, *1993*
John Thomas, owner and Lowell Nissley, manager, stand beside a 1967 Mercedes 250 SL, 6 cylinder. The 250 was basically a one year car with total production of 5,196 units. In 1994 the Museum succombed to the march of progress and is now an office building. It is located at Willow Street, Pennyslvania.

I REALLY DON'T KNOW WHAT *SPARKED* MY INTEREST (pardon the pun) in automobiles. Maybe it was an innate hydrocarbon in my blood which *steered* me in this direction. I remember when I wished for enough income to upgrade our ten-year-old car at least every three years. It was the best we could ever *Aspire* to *aFord*. But one day a member of our church offered to make it possible to get a new car! How could we ever **Dodge** such an *Intrigueing* opportunity? I visited the large storage lot (one hundred fifty cars) of a Cheverolet dealer in Kansas City, Missouri and negotiated the purchase of a black 1956 Cheverolet 150 4dr with V-8 power pac. I thought this was about the best car ever made, in fact an acquaintance told me he didn't see how the '56 Chevy could ever be improved. It was the *Altima*, the car of the *Century* yea for the *Millenia*. I always love to talk about cars often *Rambling* on and sounding just like another *air-bag*. But the *transmission* of auto history is important because cars have become a part of who we are. I discovered there existed a *universal* interest in cars among other people as well, for instance, it was inevitable that someone sometime would notice the connection between the Bible and Japanese cars: "When the disciples all came together in one *Accord*." My recent car involvement began with a public relations job at the local Peugeot dealership in Bradenton, Florida followed by a commission salesmanship job at BayView Motors in Sarasota selling antique and classic cars. It was one day here at BayView that John Thomas from Willow Valley (Lancaster, Pennsylvania) walked in. He said he recently had a bad day, not only falling off his bicycle when the handlebars came loose, but later the same day receiving a phone call from the manager of his car museum in Pennsylvania saying that he was moving and would need to terminate his position. The next day I called John and *Probed* about his future plans for his museum. The result of that conversation was four years as manager of the Thomas Antique and Classic Car Museum near Lancaster, Pennsylvania

1935 PACKARD, 1992

(1991-94). This was a great *wheel* of fortune for me. Each year the museum was closed January-March giving us three months to return to our home in Sarasota not only to maintain Florida connections but to escape Pennsylvania winters. I shall always treasure the excellent meals and outstanding beauty of Willow Valley, and the friendship of Florence and John Thomas and Emery Einreinhof, my assistant and his wife, Helen, the pushing of cars in the museum and the making of so many friends in the community and among the public. It was an experience we hold in highest *Esteem*.

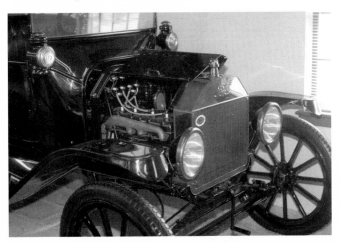

1915 FORD MODEL T, 1992

PARENTS OF THE PREACHER'S DAUGHTER, *1988*
Milton and Ruth Brackbill, Miriam's parents.

GREAT VALLEY BAPTIST CHURCH, *1908*
This is the burial site near Centerville, Pennsylvania where my mother and father are buried with many of my mother's family.

RUTH NISSLEY, *1985*
Our Daughter, Ruth, rests by her 1965 Citroen 2 CV.

JACKSON YOUNG FAMILY, *1966*
l-r: Dan, Lila, Robin, Jack. Jack worked for my father on the
Arthur Guy farm in the early 1940's. See story on pages 41-43.

FRANK BROOKS FAMILY, *1987*
l-r: Frank, Jeanette, Ronald, Stacy, Dorlene.

Frank was very helpful with this book by his eagerness to trace photographs and to document some of the missing points of genealogy. Frank Brooks' mother was Ione Smiley Brooks. Ione was my first cousin and only child of Aunt Ona and Uncle Frank Smiley. Aunt Ona was my mother's younger sister. Ione married Homer Gordy Brooks in Tampa, Florida in 1938. Frank was born in the Davis Island Hospital in Tampa January 15, 1939. In February 1947 his father tragically died by drowning in the Hillsborough River in Tampa, Florida under unknown circumstances. Frank later spent twenty three years in the Navy/Air Force where he met Dorlene Kearl. Frank and Dorlene married June 11, 1969. They live in Layton, Utah.

GREAT VALLEY BAPTIST CHURCH, 1970

SILENT SENTINAL of MEMORIES, 1970
My Grandfather's grave at the Great Valley Baptist
Church located near Centerville, Pennyslvania.

STILL PAINTING, 1972
At age ninety my father, Frank C. Nissley paints a
porch railing.

BEGINNING HIS NINTH DECADE, 1972
My father stands on the doorstep of his nintieth year.
He is at the house of the horse farm near Phoenixville,
PA where he lived after my mother's death.

Alexander (Sandy) and my sister, Naomi, were married on a very rainy day in June, 1955. The event took place on the estate in St. David's, Pennsylvania which soon after became the Eastern Baptist College campus. It was a beautiful setting with a lake, elegant landscaping and rose arbors. Unfortunately, the ceremony was interrupted three times by intermittent showers. The last one came at the point of no return with rain dripping off the minister's nose and chin as the couple said their "I dos".

NEWLY WEDS, 1955
My sister, Naomi, and Sandy enjoy some newlywed "pfun".

ALEXANDER LIMONT, PHOTOGRAPHER,
is a graduate of the Philadelphia College of Art, with graduate work at the Barnes Foundation, Merion, Pennsylvania. His field is graphic design and has been a senior art director for many years. He has done work for corporations such as SmithKline and French Laboratories (now SmithKline Beecham), and Toltzis Communications in Glenside, Pennsylvania. His work has been shown in the greater Philadelphia area, and in national magazines. He has also managed his own graphic design studio, in Philadelphia. I am especially grateful to Sandy for sharing his unusual skills in creating the format of this book!

THE AUTHOR and MIRIAM, 1997
D. Lowell and Miriam Alberta Brackbill Nissley

T HE WRITING OF THIS BOOK has been a lot of fun with more stories emerging as it went along. The strings lead off in more directions than was possible to follow. Two subjects, however, should have received more attention.

1. Education:

Miriam and I had the unique privilege of attending all three of the Mennonite Church colleges - Eastern Mennonite University, Goshen College and Hesston College. We are told these days that quality education is important for the future of our country. May I add that quality education is crucial for the future of the Mennonite Church as well, and Mennonite educational institutions need apologize to no one for their academic excellence. It's a serious concern that only 14.1 per-cent of Mennonite College students attend a Mennonite College.

2. Civilian Public Service:

CPS during WWII was not only a significant experience for the Mennonite Church, it was also for our nation. The present quality of mental health care in the United States is an outstanding case in point. It was the compassionate and caring service of the CPS men as orderlies in some of our nations' largest mental institutions that sensitized our country's conscience for improved care of the mentally ill. Since this book cannot exhaust every subject, I will leave it to others to write a history of Civilian Public Service.
Circumstances in 1995-1996 created the opportunity to re-visit several places which have impacted my life.:

COLLEGEVILLE HOUSE, PENNYSLVANIA 1997

LEMOYNE HOUSE, PENNYSLVANIA 1997

1. Collegeville, Pennsylvania. — 339 East Ninth Avenue. In October 1997 my sister, Naomi, expressed desire to look up the house in Collegeville where our parents lived seventy-seven years ago when she was born. It seemed like a wild goose chase after all these years considering the extent of urban development in recent years. However, armed only with the urgency of her request, a 1919 photo and a copy of the Pottstown Hospital maternity bill when she was born, we set out on our quest. The maternity bill said simply, "6th. Street, Collegeville". As we entered Collegeville and began searching for a Realty Office to obtain a city map, a sign at a traffic light read, "Sixth Ave." We turned left to a dead end in an upscale housing development. Following our instincts we retraced our steps and as we rounded a slight curve all exclaimed with one voice, "There it is"! Sure enough there it was - easily recognizable! The present owner, Robert W. Rosenberger has lived there since 1979. He was very gracious and invited us in and shared what history he knew. There have been few changes. He said the house was built in 1873 and was the tenant house for the farm. The small barn is now a garage.

2. Lemoyne, Pennsylvania. — 100 Walnut Avenue. One daywhen my father was in his mid-nineties, he offered to direct us to the house in Lemoyne, Pennsylvania where I was born in 1921. His directions were accurate and in spite of urban sprawl and a maze of new highways we drove right to 100 Walnut Avenue. Houses have grown up around it and the house itself has been altered somewhat by enclosing the front porch plus some other things. It is still on top of the hill overlooking the Susquehanna River and Harrisburg, Pennsylvania, the State Capital with a good view of the Capitol building. I visited there again in 1994 and took some photographs.

3. Lionville, Pennsylvania. The house is still there and looks as good or better than ever.

4. Blackhorse Hill, Pennsylvania. The house is still there but some years ago received a substantial addition. Maple trees replace the cherry trees. The field across the road leading to the woods looks like it always did, but most remarkable is the rail fence, just like we used to have, along the road with the rose bush embracing it.

5. Tampa, Florida - DeSoto Park. DeSoto Park is still there with its Pavilion and Pier and I'm sure at the right time of year, the smell of petunias. But the cottages have been replaced with ancient looking down-in-the-mouth mobile homes. The DeSoto Elementary School looks great. A nicely painted sign announces, "DeSoto Birthday Celebration 70 Years". I attended there 67 years ago.

6. Tampa, Florida - 4112 North 15th Street. The street is now blacktop instead of crushed shell. A church occupies the lot across the street where we used to play tin-can. 4112 is empty but being readied for rental. The most memorable sight was the ancient live oak still holding its ground in the front yard, with its arms stretched over the house in a kind of silent benediction.

Index of Photographs

Valley Forge House, 1923 1

Frank C. Nissley, about 1898 2

Nissley Family Portrait, 1886 3

Nissley Family Portrait, 1917 4

An Extended Nissley Family Portrait, 1919 5

Frances Kendig Nissley, about 1960 6

Abram K. McDonald, about 1960 6

Frank, A Rocker and His Paper, about 1960 6

A Gardener Forever, about 1970 6

Country School Portrait, about 1893 7

Engine Trouble? 1923 8

Collegeville House, 1919 8

Lemoyne House, 1921 9

Harrisburg From Lemoyne, 1921 9

Lionville House, 1994 10

"Downtown" Lionville, 1925 10

Nissley Homestead, 1994 11

Little Giant in Nebraska Mud, 1915 11

Frank C. Nissley, "Business Man", about 1905 12

A Mobile Photo Studio, 1915 12

Mary McCloskey, 1857 13

Sampler, late 1700's 13

Orphan, Mary Madden, 1863 14

John M. Madden, about 1864 15

John M. Madden's Journals,1860 16

Joseph Madden, early 1860's 17

Mary Josephine Bogia Madden, about 1920 18

Extended Madden Family Portrait, 1923 19

Madden Family Portrait, about 1920 20

Haunted House, 1970 21

My Mother, A Teenager, 1898 22

Harry S. Miller, about 1895 23

My Mother, 1908 23

Miller Family Portrait, 1906 23

Grace and Charles Miller, about 1914 24

Brother and Sister, 1908 24

Ruth Miller in Casket, 1911 24

Henry Rutter in Casket, 1909 24

Mary Jessica Madden, My Mother, about 1885 25

My Mother, 1908 25

My Mother in Her Florida Bathing Suit, 1911 25

"Alone", 1911 26

A-Soon-To-Be-Bride, 1918 26

My Mother, 1950 26

Will Chronister, 1913 27

Will Chronister and His 1903 Rambler, 1903 27

Elizabeth Ann Nell Chronister, 1920's 28

Smiley Family Portrait, around 1920 28

Retouching Photos, about 1917 29

Before Shamokin Fire, 1916 29

After The Shamokin Fire, 1916 30

Collage 31-32

Cupie Doll, 1923 33

School Daze, 1930 33

Three Siblings, 1921 33

White Fences, 1994 34

Happy Artist, 1980 34

Potato Harvest, 1926 35

Blackhorse Hill House, 1928 36

Blackhill House, 1994 37

Lionville Barn, 1926 38

St. Matthew's School, 1995 39

Ready To Roll, 1918 40

Arthur Guy Farm, 1930's 41

Home On The Arthur Guy Farm, 1938 42

That's A Lot of Hay, 1938 43

Naomi's first Christmas, 1919 44

My First Christmas, 1921 45

Naomi's second Christmas, 1920 45

Christmas, 1922 46

Christmas, 1923 46

Christmas, 1924 47

St. Matthews Church, 1994 47

St Matthews School Portrait, 1930 48

Uncle Charles and Aunt Ruth Boyer, 1890's 49

"Watch The Birdie", Fall 1921 49

Cousins, late 1920's 50

Cousins, about 1925 50

Cousins, late 1920's 51
Laurie Madden, about 1915 51
Laurie Madden, about 1920 51
My First Pony Ride, 1929 52
"Giddyup", about 1925 52
Three KKK Sisters, 1925 53
Ku Lux Klan, 1926 53
Light Snow in Birmingham, 1917 54
Desoto Elementry School, 1995 55
Our Housecar Trailer, 1933 55
A Few Friends, 1933 55
Swimming Hole, 1933 56
Upstairs Florida Apartment, 1918 56
4112 N. 15th. St. Tampa, Florida, 1932 57
4112 N. 15th. St. Tampa, Florida, 1996 57
Deep Diver, 1933 58
Pack-Up Time, 1928 58
Time To Take it Easy, 1917 59
Stone Moutain, Georgia, 1917 59
My Mother's 1916 Pullman, 1917 59
Oranges In Florida, 1917 60
My Father with his 1916 Pullman, 1917 60
Florida's Best, 1928 61
A Good Catch, 1928 61
Live Oak, about 1928 61
Levi and Ella Glick, 1933 62
Ida Mennonoite Church and Parsonage, 1933 63
"Mutt and Jeff", 1936 64
My Grandmother's Confirmation, 1892 65
My Mother's Certificate of Baptism, 1893 65
My Certificate of Infant Baptism, 1923 65
Eastern Mennonite College, 1940 66
Eastern Mennonite School, 1937 66
Hillsborourg High School, 1995 67
Cheerleaders, 1938 67
Hillsborough High School Senior, 1938 68
Ninth Grade Graduate, 1936 68
High School Prom, 1938 68
Paul DuBois Miller, My Half-Brother, 1930's 69
Miller Family Portrait, 1940 69
My Family, 1942 70
Paul Miller Family, 1988 70
Camping Out, 1923 71
Motor Home, 1923 72
Family Camping, 1923 73
No Interstate, 1917 74
Gas & Oil Delivery, 1918 75
Larry Madden Milk Delivery, 1916 75
A Coal Miner's Son 76
Blind Peddler 76
General J.B.Carr 77
Verdent Wood 77
Still Waters 78
Flood Reflections 78
I Love You 79
Our Future 79
Boy and His Dog 80
How Do I Look? 80
She's A Doll 80
Somber Faces 81
42 States 82
Eastern Star 82
Holstein Herd, 1989 83
Liberty Bell, 1946 83
I Was A Tree Surgeon, 1941 84
Women's Section, 1940 85
Men's Section, 1940 85
Civilian Public Service #45, 1943 86
Dignified Campers Pose With A Special Guest, ... 86
Fire Fighting Crew and Truck, 1943 87
Abandoned Mountain Cemetery, 1943 87
Orchard Crew, 1943 87
Typical Mountain Terrain, 1943 88
Big Meadows Nursery Crew, 1943 88
Getting ready For Winter, 1942 88
D.H.I.A. Technitions, 1944 89
Get The Drift?, 1941 90
Some New Wilmington Friends, 1944 90

Index of Photographs

The Preacher's Daughter, 1928 92

Neat Date Place,1941 92

Varden Leasa, 1996 92

Brackbill Family, 1966 93

Our Marriage Certificate, 1947 94

Our Official Wedding Picture, 1947 94

Happy Camper, 1947 94

Honey Moon Campsite, 1947 94

"Oakwood" Ground Breaking, 1950 95

Jubilee Class, 1995 96

Crystal Springs Mennonite Church, 1951 97

The Preacher's Daughter, 1934 98

Crystal Springs, Kansas, 1971 99

Church Sign, 1953 99

Jay Whitwill, 1950's 100

Argentine Mennonite Church, 1955 101

Grace Mennonite Church, 1960 103

Grace Mennonite Church Interior, 1960 104

Charter Members, Grace Youth Fellowship, 1958 105

First Pastor's Council, 1958 105

Our Family, 1956 105

I Was A Truck Driver, 3/27/73 106

Cypress Gardens, 1948 107

Bok Yower, Florida, 1948 108

An Academic Setting, 1949 108

Jan Gleysteen, 1988 109

Ruth Anita Nissley, 1992 110

Dale Richard Nissley, 1996 110

Our Grandchildren, 1991 111

Dale Nissley Family, 1996 111

The Author, Miriam and Ruth, 1997 112

Frank C. Nissley, My Father, 1957 113

Mary Jessica Madden Nissley, My Mother, 1958 114

Nissley/DuBois Family Time Line 115-116

Thomas Antique & Classic Car Museum, 1993 117

1935 Packard, 1992 118

1915 Model T Ford, 1992 118

Parents of The Preacher's Daughter, 1988 119

Great Valley Baptist Church, 1908 119

Ruth Nissley, 1985 119

Jackson Young Family, 1966 120

Frank Brooks Family, 1987 120

Silent Sentinel of Memories, 1970 121

Great Valley Baptist Church, 1970 121

Still Painting, 1972 121

Begining His Ninth Decade, 1972 121

Newly Weds, 1955 122

Alexander Limont, Photographer 122

The Author & Miriam, 1997 123

Collegeville House, Pennyslvania, 1997 124

Lemoyne House, Pennyslvania, 1997 124